# TOWARDS SUSTAINABLE DEVELOPMENT

# ENVIRONMENTAL INDICATORS

ORGANISATION FOR ECONOMIC CO-OPERATION AND DEVELOPMENT

# ORGANISATION FOR ECONOMIC CO-OPERATION AND DEVELOPMENT

Pursuant to Article 1 of the Convention signed in Paris on 14th December 1960, and which came into force on 30th September 1961, the Organisation for Economic Co-operation and Development (OECD) shall promote policies designed:

- to achieve the highest sustainable economic growth and employment and a rising standard of living in Member countries, while maintaining financial stability, and thus to contribute to the development of the world economy;
- to contribute to sound economic expansion in Member as well as non-member countries in the process of economic development; and
- to contribute to the expansion of world trade on a multilateral, non-discriminatory basis in accordance with international obligations.

The original Member countries of the OECD are Austria, Belgium, Canada, Denmark, France, Germany, Greece, Iceland, Ireland, Italy, Luxembourg, the Netherlands, Norway, Portugal, Spain, Sweden, Switzerland, Turkey, the United Kingdom and the United States. The following countries became Members subsequently through accession at the dates indicated hereafter: Japan (28th April 1964), Finland (28th January 1969), Australia (7th June 1971), New Zealand (29th May 1973), Mexico (18th May 1994), the Czech Republic (21st December 1995), Hungary (7th May 1996), Poland (22nd November 1996) and Korea (12th December 1996). The Commission of the European Communities takes part in the work of the OECD (Article 13 of the OECD Convention).

Publié en français sous le titre :

VERS UN DÉVELOPPEMENT DURABLE
**INDICATEURS D'ENVIRONNEMENT**

Reprinted 1998

# FOREWORD

In recent years, concerns about whether development is sustainable from an economic, environmental and social point of view have prompted a number of countries to further move towards policies focusing on pollution prevention, integration of environmental concerns in economic and sectoral decisions, and international co-operation. There is also increasing interest in evaluating how well governments are implementing their policies and how well they are satisfying their domestic objectives and international commitments. These demands have led to the development of environmental indicators as a tool for decision making and for assessing countries' environmental performance.

The OECD work programme on environmental indicators has led to several sets of indicators each responding to a specific purpose: an OECD Core Set of environmental indicators to measure environmental progress, and various sets of indicators to integrate environmental concerns in sectoral policies (e.g. energy, transport, agriculture). Indicators are also derived from natural resource and environmental expenditure accounts.

The present report is one of the products of this OECD work programme on environmental indicators. It includes leading environmental indicators, as well as selected socio-economic and sectoral indicators having an environmental significance. It highlights the linkages between environmental indicators, environmental performance and sustainable development, and thus provides a building block for the environmental component of sustainable development indicators.

This report was prepared by the OECD Secretariat, but its successful completion depended on personal or official contributions by many individuals in Member countries, and on the work and support of the OECD Group on the State of the Environment. This report is published on the responsibility of the Secretary General of the OECD.

*Data in this report largely come from "OECD Environmental Data - Compendium 1997". These data are harmonised through the work of the OECD Group on the State of the Environment (SOE). Some were updated or revised on the basis of comments from SOE Delegates, as received by 27 February 1998.*

*In many countries, systematic collection of environmental data has a short history; sources are typically spread across a range of agencies and levels of government, and information is often collected for other purposes. When reading this report, one should therefore keep in mind that definitions and measurement methods vary among countries and that intercountry comparisons require great caution. One should also note that indicators presented in this report refer to the national level and may conceal major subnational differences.*

# TABLE OF CONTENTS

# I.    INTRODUCTION

# THE OECD WORK ON ENVIRONMENTAL INDICATORS

**PURPOSES**

The OECD programme on environmental indicators has three major purposes:

♦ keeping track of environmental progress;

♦ ensuring that environmental concerns are taken into account when policies are formulated and implemented for various sectors, such as transport, energy and agriculture;

♦ ensuring similar integration of environmental concerns into economic policies, mainly through environmental accounting.

**CONCRETE RESULTS[1]**

The work on indicators is carried out in close co-operation with OECD Member countries. It has led to:

♦ agreement by OECD countries to use the pressure-state-response (PSR) model as a common harmonised framework;

♦ identification and definition of several sets of indicators based on their policy relevance, analytical soundness and measurability;

♦ measurement and publication of these indicators for a number of countries.

The results of this work, and in particular its conceptual framework, have in turn influenced similar activities by countries and international organisations (e.g the UNCSD, with its work on sustainable development indicators).

**USES**

The OECD's environmental indicators are regularly used in *environmental performance reviews*; they are a valuable way to monitor the integration of economic and environmental decision making, to analyse environmental policies and to gauge the results. Beyond their immediate application in OECD environmental performance reviews, these indicators also contribute to the broader objective of *reporting on sustainable development*.

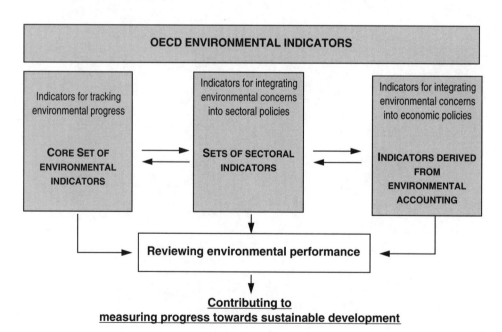

1. For further details on the OECD framework for environmental indicators, see page 105.

## THE OECD SETS OF ENVIRONMENTAL INDICATORS

**TRACKING PROGRESS: THE OECD CORE SET OF ENVIRONMENTAL INDICATORS**

The OECD Core Set of environmental indicators is a commonly agreed upon, minimum set of indicators for OECD countries and for international use, published regularly. It is a first step in tracking environmental progress and the factors involved in it.

The Core Set, averaging 50 indicators, covers issues that reflect the main environmental concerns in OECD countries. It incorporates major indicators derived from sectoral sets as well as from environmental accounting. Indicators are classified following the PSR model: i) indicators of environmental pressures, both direct and indirect; ii) indicators of environmental conditions; and iii) indicators of society's responses.

**PROMOTING INTEGRATION: OECD SECTORAL INDICATORS**

In addition, OECD sets of sectoral indicators focus on specific sectors (e.g. energy, transport, agriculture). Indicators are classified following an adjusted PSR model: i) sectoral trends of environmental significance and related driving forces, ii) their interactions with the environment and natural resources, including positive and negative effects, and iii) related economic and policy considerations.

**PROMOTING INTEGRATION: ENVIRONMENTAL ACCOUNTING**

Environmental indicators are also derived from the OECD work on environmental accounting focusing on i) physical natural resource accounts, which help in efforts to achieve sustainable management of natural resources, and ii) environmental expenditure. Examples of these indicators are the level and structure of pollution abatement and control expenditure and the intensity of natural resource use.

## THE 1998 PUBLICATION

**CONTENT**

The present publication provides a follow-up to the 1994 publication "Environmental indicators - OECD Core Set". It presents major indicators from the Core Set as well as selected socio-economic and sectoral indicators with environmental significance. It highlights links among environmental indicators, environmental performance and sustainable development, and thus is a building block for the environmental component of sustainable development indicators.

**STRUCTURE**

The publication is in five parts:

♦ Part I is an introduction to the publication;

♦ Part II presents major environmental indicators of the OECD Core Set grouped by environmental issue;

♦ Part III presents selected socio-economic indicators with environmental significance. A number of these are derived from the OECD's work on sectoral indicators;

♦ Part IV describes the OECD framework for environmental indicators;

♦ Part V, a Technical Annex, includes data sources, notes and comments on the indicators and on underlying data sets.

Each section of indicators includes:

♦ a brief statement on the issue referred to and its importance for environmental performance and sustainable development;

♦ an overview of related OECD work and references, including a schematic description of the conceptual framework in which the indicators are placed (i.e. the PSR model for OECD Core Set indicators and the adjusted PSR model for OECD sectoral indicators);

♦ a summary of major trends.

The indicators in this publication are those that are regularly used in the OECD's analytical work and for which data are available for a majority of OECD countries. They are of varying relevance for different countries and have to be interpreted in context.

**DATA**     The internationally harmonised data used to calculate the indicators are based on those published in "OECD Environmental Data - Compendium 1997" and on comments received from Member countries before 27 February 1998. The data come from the OECD SIREN database, which is regularly updated with information from Member countries (through biennial data collection using the OECD/Eurostat questionnaires on the state of the environment and on pollution abatement and control expenditure), from internal OECD sources and from other international sources.

## PROSPECTS AND FUTURE WORK

The OECD experience shows that environmental indicators are cost-effective and powerful tools for tracking and charting environmental progress and measuring environmental performance. However, experience also shows significant lags between the demand for environmental indicators, the related conceptual work and the actual capacity for mobilising and validating underlying data. In the field of environmental statistics, differences among countries may be considerable and the establishment of reliable and internationally comparable data calls for continuous monitoring, analysis, treatment and checking.

Following the conceptual work that laid down the common framework and basic principles for developing sets of international environmental indicators in the OECD context, progress is now needed in:

♦ improving the quality and comparability of existing indicators;

♦ linking the indicators more closely to established goals and commitments;

♦ further integrating environmental and sectoral indicator sets in a broader set of sustainable development indicators.

This necessitates greater policy relevance and increased quality and timeliness of basic data sets, as well as a closer link between environmental data and existing economic and social information systems. Continued work is being done by the OECD to further improve and harmonise these data, and to develop a second generation of indicators.

# II.    ENVIRONMENTAL INDICATORS

# CLIMATE CHANGE

*Industrialisation has increased emissions of greenhouses gases (GHG) from human activities, disturbing the radiative energy balance of the earth-atmosphere system. These gases exacerbate the natural greenhouse effect, leading to temperature changes and other potential consequences for the earth's climate. Land use changes and forestry also contribute to the greenhouse effect by altering carbon sinks. Climate change is of concern mainly as relates to its impact on ecosystems (biodiversity), human settlements and agriculture, and possible consequences for other socio-economic activities that could affect global economic output.*

*Climate change could have major or significant effects on <u>sustainable development</u>. <u>Performance</u> can be assessed against domestic objectives and international commitments. The overall objective of the United Nations Framework Convention on Climate Change (FCCC) (Rio de Janeiro, 1992) is to stabilise GHG concentrations in the atmosphere at a level that would prevent dangerous anthropogenic interference with the climate system. The FCCC has been ratified by 171 parties. Industrialised countries, including those in transition to market economies, are committed to taking measures aimed at stabilising GHG emissions by 2000 at 1990 levels. The Kyoto Protocol establishes legally binding, differentiated national or regional emission reduction or limitation targets for industrialised countries for 2008-12. The targets are comprehensive, covering $CO_2$, $CH_4$, $N_2O$, PFCs, HFCs and $SF_6$.*

*<u>Indicators</u> presented here relate to:*

- ♦ *<u>$CO_2$ emissions from energy use</u>, showing total emissions as well as <u>emission intensities</u> per unit of GDP and per capita, and related changes since 1980. $CO_2$ from combustion of fossil fuels and biomass is a major contributor to the greenhouse effect and a key factor in countries' ability to deal with climate change. In the absence of national inventories that provide a complete and consistent picture of all GHG emissions, energy-related $CO_2$ emissions are used to reflect overall trends in direct GHG emissions. All emissions presented here are gross direct emissions, excluding sinks and indirect effects. Information on fossil fuel share and intensity is given to reflect, at least partly, changes in energy efficiency and energy mix, which are key in efforts to reduce atmospheric $CO_2$ emissions.*

- ♦ *atmospheric <u>concentrations of the greenhouse gases</u> covered by the FCCC ($CO_2$, $CH_4$, $N_2O$) and of selected ozone depleting substances controlled by the Montreal Protocol (page 19) that also play a role in the greenhouse effect (CFC-11, CFC-12, total gaseous chlorine). Data are from various monitoring sites that provide an indication of global concentrations and trends.*

*These indicators can be related to trends in GDP, energy intensity, the structure of energy supply and the relative importance of fossil fuels, as well as to energy prices and taxes.*

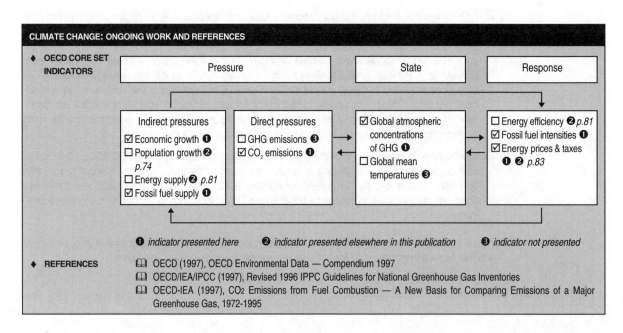

CLIMATE CHANGE: ONGOING WORK AND REFERENCES

♦ OECD CORE SET INDICATORS

| Pressure | State | Response |
|---|---|---|

| Indirect pressures | Direct pressures | ☑ Global atmospheric concentrations of GHG ❶ <br> ☐ Global mean temperatures ❸ | ☐ Energy efficiency ❷ *p.81* <br> ☑ Fossil fuel intensities ❶ <br> ☑ Energy prices & taxes ❶ ❷ *p.83* |
|---|---|---|---|
| ☑ Economic growth ❶ <br> ☐ Population growth ❷ *p.74* <br> ☐ Energy supply ❷ *p.81* <br> ☑ Fossil fuel supply ❶ | ☐ GHG emissions ❸ <br> ☑ $CO_2$ emissions ❶ | | |

❶ *indicator presented here*    ❷ *indicator presented elsewhere in this publication*    ❸ *indicator not presented*

♦ REFERENCES

 📖 OECD (1997), OECD Environmental Data — Compendium 1997

 📖 OECD/IEA/IPCC (1997), Revised 1996 IPPC Guidelines for National Greenhouse Gas Inventories

 📖 OECD-IEA (1997), $CO_2$ Emissions from Fuel Combustion — A New Basis for Comparing Emissions of a Major Greenhouse Gas, 1972-1995

## CO₂ EMISSION INTENSITIES ▮1▮

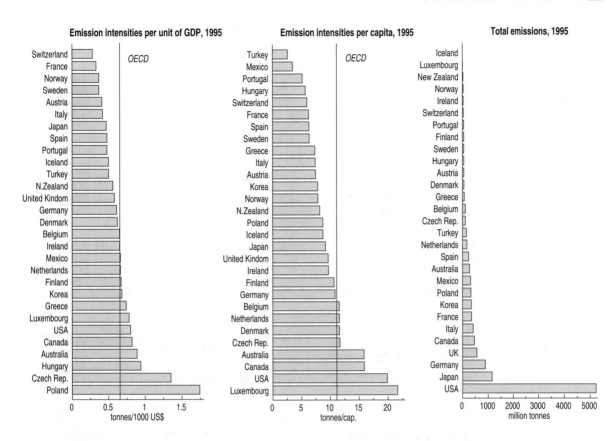

**Emission intensities per unit of GDP, 1995** — tonnes/1000 US$

**Emission intensities per capita, 1995** — tonnes/cap.

**Total emissions, 1995** — million tonnes

### Contribution of OECD countries to world emissions

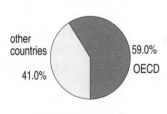

other countries 41.0%

OECD 59.0%

**World 1980 emissions
18 billion tonnes**

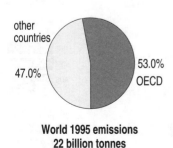

other countries 47.0%

OECD 53.0%

**World 1995 emissions
22 billion tonnes**

### Structure of OECD emissions

1980 | 22% | 36% | 24% | 18% | 11 billion tonnes

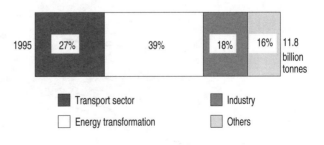

1995 | 27% | 39% | 18% | 16% | 11.8 billion tonnes

- ■ Transport sector
- ■ Industry
- □ Energy transformation
- ▨ Others

*N.B. Data refer to CO₂ emissions from energy use.*

*OECD Environmental Indicators 1998*

# 1 CO₂ EMISSION INTENSITIES

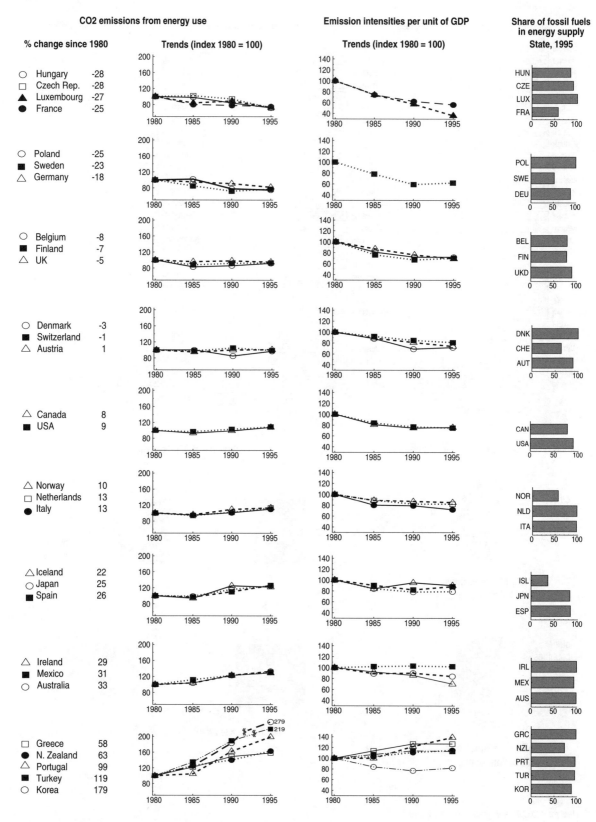

CO2 emissions from energy use

% change since 1980

Emission intensities per unit of GDP

Share of fossil fuels in energy supply
State, 1995

Trends (index 1980 = 100)

| | | |
|---|---|---|
| ○ | Hungary | -28 |
| □ | Czech Rep. | -28 |
| ▲ | Luxembourg | -27 |
| ● | France | -25 |

| | | |
|---|---|---|
| ○ | Poland | -25 |
| ■ | Sweden | -23 |
| △ | Germany | -18 |

| | | |
|---|---|---|
| ○ | Belgium | -8 |
| ■ | Finland | -7 |
| △ | UK | -5 |

| | | |
|---|---|---|
| ○ | Denmark | -3 |
| ■ | Switzerland | -1 |
| △ | Austria | 1 |

| | | |
|---|---|---|
| △ | Canada | 8 |
| ■ | USA | 9 |

| | | |
|---|---|---|
| △ | Norway | 10 |
| □ | Netherlands | 13 |
| ● | Italy | 13 |

| | | |
|---|---|---|
| △ | Iceland | 22 |
| ○ | Japan | 25 |
| ■ | Spain | 26 |

| | | |
|---|---|---|
| △ | Ireland | 29 |
| ■ | Mexico | 31 |
| ○ | Australia | 33 |

| | | |
|---|---|---|
| □ | Greece | 58 |
| ● | N. Zealand | 63 |
| △ | Portugal | 99 |
| ■ | Turkey | 119 |
| ○ | Korea | 179 |

## CO$_2$ EMISSION INTENSITIES 1

| | CO$_2$ emissions from energy use | | | | | | | Fossil fuel supply | | Real end-use energy prices | GDP |
|---|---|---|---|---|---|---|---|---|---|---|---|
| | Total | | | Emission intensities | | | | Share of total supply | Intensity per unit of GDP | | |
| | | | | per unit of GDP | | per capita | | | | | |
| | million tonnes 1995 | % change since 1980 | % change since 1990 | t/1 000 US$ 1995 | % change since1980 | tonnes/cap. 1995 | % change since1980 | % 1995 | Toe/1 000 US$ 1995 | % change since 1980 | % change since 1980 |
| Canada | 471 | 8 | 9 | 0.821 | -24 | 15.9 | -10 | 77 | 0.41 | -1 | 43 |
| Mexico ♦ | 328 | 31 | 6 | 0.657 | 2 | 3.5 | -4 | 93 | 0.27 | *61* | 29 |
| USA | 5229 | 9 | 7 | 0.797 | -25 | 19.9 | -5 | 89 | 0.32 | -38 | 46 |
| Japan | 1151 | 25 | 8 | 0.470 | -21 | 9.2 | 17 | 83 | 0.20 | -47 | 59 |
| Korea | 353 | 179 | 52 | 0.680 | -18 | 7.8 | 136 | 88 | 0.28 | -31 | 241 |
| Australia | 286 | 33 | 8 | 0.885 | -16 | 15.8 | 8 | 98 | 0.29 | -6 | 57 |
| New Zealand | 29 | 63 | 16 | 0.562 | 15 | 8.2 | 43 | 73 | 0.30 | -29 | 41 |
| Austria | 60 | 1 | 1 | 0.412 | -26 | 7.5 | -5 | 88 | 0.18 | -33 | 37 |
| Belgium | 117 | - 8 | 7 | 0.648 | -28 | 11.6 | -11 | 79 | 0.29 | -30 | 28 |
| Czech Rep. | 120 | - 28 | - 23 | 1.347 | .. | 11.7 | -28 | 91 | 0.44 | 49 | .. |
| Denmark | 61 | - 3 | 14 | 0.618 | -28 | 11.6 | -5 | 99 | 0.21 | -19 | 35 |
| Finland | 54 | - 7 | 1 | 0.673 | -30 | 10.6 | -13 | 78 | 0.35 | -30 | 32 |
| France | 362 | - 25 | - 4 | 0.333 | -44 | 6.2 | -31 | 58 | 0.22 | -26 | 33 |
| Germany | 884 | - 18 | - 10 | 0.614 | .. | 10.8 | -22 | 88 | 0.24 | -31 | .. |
| Greece | 77 | 58 | 6 | 0.742 | 27 | 7.3 | 46 | 98 | 0.23 | -24 | 24 |
| Hungary | 58 | - 28 | - 15 | 0.937 | .. | 5.6 | -25 | 85 | 0.41 | 18 | .. |
| Iceland | 2 | 22 | - 2 | 0.495 | -10 | 8.8 | 4 | 36 | 0.45 | .. | 36 |
| Ireland | 35 | 29 | 5 | 0.654 | -30 | 9.7 | 22 | 99 | 0.21 | -31 | 84 |
| Italy | 424 | 13 | 4 | 0.417 | -15 | 7.4 | 11 | 97 | 0.16 | -2 | 32 |
| Luxembourg | 9 | - 27 | - 18 | 0.778 | -64 | 21.6 | -35 | 100 | 0.29 | -22 | 100 |
| Netherlands | 179 | 13 | 11 | 0.665 | -18 | 11.6 | 3 | 98 | 0.27 | -9 | 38 |
| Norway | 34 | 10 | 9 | 0.375 | -28 | 7.9 | 3 | 57 | 0.26 | 36 | 52 |
| Poland | 336 | - 25 | - 4 | 1.736 | .. | 8.7 | -31 | 100 | 0.51 | .. | .. |
| Portugal | 51 | 99 | 22 | 0.484 | 39 | 5.1 | 97 | 96 | 0.18 | -44 | 43 |
| Spain | 247 | 26 | 14 | 0.477 | -12 | 6.3 | 20 | 84 | 0.20 | -16 | 44 |
| Sweden | 56 | - 23 | 6 | 0.375 | -38 | 6.3 | -28 | 52 | 0.34 | -5 | 24 |
| Switzerland | 42 | - 1 | - 5 | 0.284 | -19 | 5.9 | -10 | 63 | 0.17 | -45 | 23 |
| Turkey | 160 | 119 | 16 | 0.504 | 13 | 2.6 | 58 | 95 | 0.20 | -10 | 94 |
| UK | 565 | - 5 | - 3 | 0.578 | -31 | 9.6 | -9 | 89 | 0.23 | -23 | 38 |
| OECD | 11780 | 7 | 5 | 0.650 | .. | 10.9 | -5 | 86 | 0.27 | -28 | .. |
| World | 22150 | 18 | 4 | .. | .. | 3.9 | -7 | .. | .. | .. | .. |

♦ *See Technical Annex for data sources, notes and comments.*

**STATE AND TRENDS SUMMARY**

Despite wide variations in emission trends, most OECD countries have *decoupled* their CO$_2$ emissions from GDP growth through structural changes in industry and in energy supply and the gradual improvement of energy efficiency in production processes.

CO$_2$ and other GHG emissions are still growing in many countries and overall. Since 1980, CO$_2$ emissions from energy use have grown more slowly in OECD countries as a group than they have worldwide. Individual OECD countries' contributions to the greenhouse effect, and rates of progress towards stabilisation, vary significantly.

CO$_2$ emissions from energy use *continue to grow,* particularly in the OECD Asia-Pacific region and in North America. This can be partly attributed to energy production and consumption patterns and trends, often combined with low energy prices. In OECD Europe, by contrast, CO$_2$ emissions from energy use have *fallen* since 1980 on a combination of changes in economic structures and energy supply mix, energy savings and, in a few countries, decreases in economic activity.

## 2 GREENHOUSE GAS CONCENTRATIONS

### Gases controlled under the Framework Convention on Climate Change

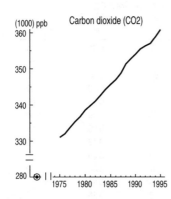
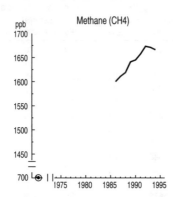
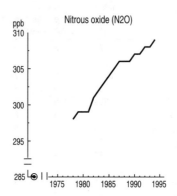

### Gases controlled under the Montreal Protocol (subst. depleting the ozone layer)

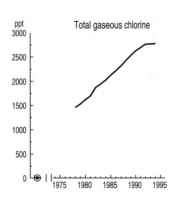
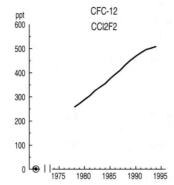
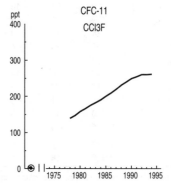

⊚ - Preindustrial level

**STATE AND TRENDS
SUMMARY**

Since the beginning of industrialisation, human activity has substantially raised atmospheric concentrations of GHG. Global $CO_2$ concentrations have increased along with world population. According to the IPCC (1996), global mean surface air temperature has increased by between 0.3 and 0.6 degree Celsius since the 19th century and is expected to rise 1° to 3.5°C in the 21st century.

Trends also show large increases in concentrations of ozone depleting substances (ODS) in the atmosphere. A number of ODS play a role in the greenhouse effect. However, growth rates of CFC concentrations have decreased since 1989 as a result of the Montreal Protocol and its amendments. (see also page 19)

# OZONE LAYER DEPLETION

*The release into the atmosphere of certain man-made substances containing chlorine and bromine endangers the stratospheric ozone layer, which shields the earth's surface from ultraviolet radiation. This raises concerns regarding human health, crop yields and the natural environment. The main ozone depleting substances (ODS) are CFCs, halons, methyl chloroform, carbon tetrachloride, HCFCs and methyl bromide. These are man-made chemicals which have been used in air conditioning and refrigeration equipment, aerosol sprays, foamed plastics, and fire extinguishers. They are also used as solvents and pesticides.*

*The depletion of the ozone layer could have major or significant effects on <u>sustainable development</u>. <u>Performance</u> can be assessed against domestic objectives and international commitments. The major international agreements in this area are the Convention for the Protection of the Ozone Layer (Vienna, 1985), the Montreal Protocol (1987) and subsequent London (1990) and Copenhagen (1992) Amendments on substances that deplete the ozone layer. The protocol and amendments set out timetables for phasing out ODS. The Montreal Protocol has been ratified by 165 parties, including all OECD countries. Countries are developing alternatives to or substitutes for ODS, recovering and recycling ODS and regulating the emissions of ODS.*

*<u>Indicators</u> presented here relate to:*

♦ *<u>ozone depleting substances</u>, i.e. the production and consumption of CFCs, halons and HCFCs, and the production of methyl bromide*

♦ *<u>stratospheric ozone levels</u> expressed as the values of total ozone in a vertical atmospheric column over selected stations in OECD cities, presented with a zonal average (from 70N to 70S) taken from satellite data to put trends from individual stations in a global context.*

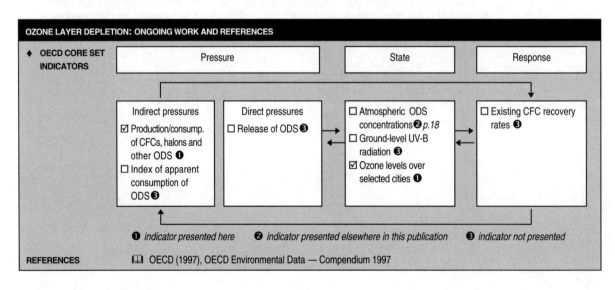

## OZONE DEPLETING SUBSTANCES **3**

### Production of CFCs and halons

North America (CAN+USA)

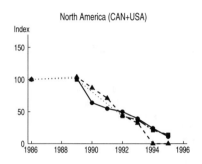

EU-15

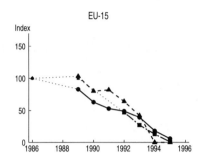

Japan

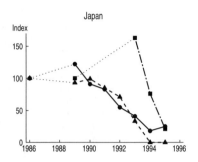

OECD (non article 5)

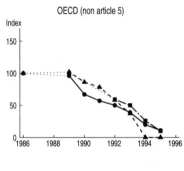

OECD (article 5: MEX+KOR+TUR)

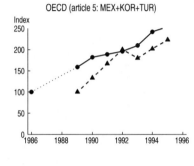

● **CFCs** (1986=100)      ▲ **Halons** (1986=100)      ■ **Other CFCs** (1989=100)

### Production of HCFCs and methyl bromide

North America (CAN+USA)

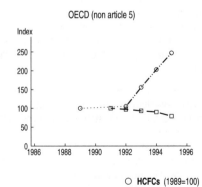

EU-15

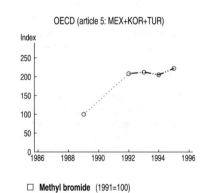

Japan

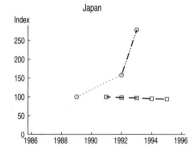

OECD (non article 5)

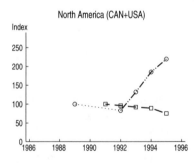

OECD (article 5: MEX+KOR+TUR)

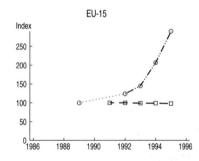

○ **HCFCs** (1989=100)      □ **Methyl bromide** (1991=100)

# 3 OZONE DEPLETING SUBSTANCES

| | Production | | | | | | Consumption | | | | | | Consumption per capita | | |
|---|---|---|---|---|---|---|---|---|---|---|---|---|---|---|---|
| | CFCs | | Halons | | HCFCs | | CFCs | | Halons | | HCFCs | | CFCs | HCFCs | Total |
| | ODP tonnes 1995 | Change (%) 1986-95 | ODP tonnes 1995 | Change (%) 1986-95 | ODP tonnes 1995 | Change (%) 1989-95 | ODP tonnes 1995 | Change (%) 1986-95 | ODP tonnes 1995 | Change (%) 1986-95 | ODP tonnes 1995 | Change (%) 1989-95 | 1995 kg/cap. | 1995 kg/cap. | 1995 kg/cap. |
| Canada | 0 | - 100 | 0 | .. | 59 | - 76 | 4 816 | - 76 | 0 | - 100 | 642 | 76 | 0.16 | 0.02 | 0.18 |
| Mexico | 15 737 | 83 | 0 | .. | 118 | 91 | 4 859 | - 45 | 0 | - 100 | 314 | 320 | 0.05 | - | 0.05 |
| USA | 34 728 | - 89 | 0 | - 100 | 14 893 | 127 | 35 530 | - 88 | 0 | - 100 | 14 023 | 120 | 0.14 | 0.05 | 0.19 |
| Japan | 29 757 | - 75 | 0 | - 100 | .. | .. | 23 064 | - 80 | 0 | - 100 | .. | .. | 0.18 | .. | .. |
| Korea | 9 746 | 594 | 3 400 | .. | 307 | 137 | 10 039 | 18 | 3 400 | 16 | 660 | 195 | 0.22 | 0.01 | 0.31 |
| Australia | 3 850 | - 75 | 0 | .. | 85 | - 36 | 2 585 | - 82 | 0 | - 100 | 156 | 5 | 0.14 | 0.01 | 0.15 |
| New Zealand | 0 | .. | 0 | .. | 0 | .. | 189 | - 91 | 0 | - 100 | 40 | 76 | 0.05 | 0.01 | 0.06 |
| Austria | 0 | .. | 0 | .. | 0 | .. | .. | .. | .. | .. | .. | .. | .. | .. | .. |
| Belgium | 0 | .. | 0 | .. | 0 | .. | .. | .. | .. | .. | .. | .. | .. | .. | .. |
| Czech Rep. | 320 | - 84 | 0 | .. | 0 | .. | 369 | - 93 | 3 | - 97 | 54 | 2 872 | 0.04 | 0.01 | 0.04 |
| Denmark | 0 | .. | 0 | .. | 0 | .. | 1 | - 100 | .. | .. | .. | .. | - | .. | .. |
| Finland | 0 | .. | 0 | .. | 0 | .. | 61 | - 98 | 0 | - 100 | 58 | 187 | 0.01 | 0.01 | 0.02 |
| France | 244 | - 100 | 0 | - 100 | 5 798 | 632 | .. | .. | .. | .. | .. | .. | .. | .. | .. |
| Germany | 0 | - 100 | 0 | - 100 | 642 | 25 | .. | .. | .. | .. | .. | .. | .. | .. | .. |
| Greece | 2 453 | - 83 | 0 | .. | 377 | 400 | .. | .. | .. | .. | .. | .. | .. | .. | .. |
| Hungary | 0 | .. | 0 | .. | 0 | .. | 566 | - 90 | 0 | - 100 | 61 | 60 800 | 0.06 | 0.01 | 0.06 |
| Iceland | 0 | .. | 0 | .. | 0 | .. | 0 | - 100 | 0 | - 100 | 8 | 58 | - | 0.03 | 0.03 |
| Ireland | 0 | .. | 0 | .. | 0 | .. | .. | .. | .. | .. | .. | .. | .. | .. | .. |
| Italy | 5 931 | - 90 | 0 | - 100 | 670 | 99 | .. | .. | .. | .. | .. | .. | .. | .. | .. |
| Luxembourg | 0 | .. | 0 | .. | 0 | .. | .. | .. | .. | .. | .. | .. | .. | .. | .. |
| Netherlands | 10 417 | - 75 | 0 | .. | 844 | 64 | 916 | - 98 | .. | .. | .. | .. | 0.06 | .. | .. |
| Norway | 0 | .. | 0 | .. | 0 | .. | 3 | - 100 | 0 | - 100 | 53 | 5 | - | 0.01 | 0.01 |
| Poland | 0 | .. | 0 | .. | .. | .. | 1 756 | - 65 | 0 | - 100 | .. | .. | 0.05 | .. | .. |
| Portugal | 0 | .. | 0 | .. | 0 | .. | .. | .. | .. | .. | .. | .. | .. | .. | .. |
| Spain | 5 435 | - 84 | 0 | .. | 741 | 54 | .. | .. | .. | .. | .. | .. | .. | .. | .. |
| Sweden | 0 | .. | 0 | .. | 0 | .. | .. | .. | .. | .. | .. | .. | .. | .. | .. |
| Switzerland | 0 | .. | 0 | .. | 0 | .. | 275 | - 97 | .. | .. | 58 | 221 | 0.04 | 0.01 | .. |
| Turkey | 0 | .. | 0 | .. | 0 | .. | 3 789 | - 8 | 88 | - 30 | 61 | 209 | 0.06 | - | 0.06 |
| UK | 4 029 | - 96 | 0 | - 100 | 1 368 | 54 | .. | .. | .. | .. | .. | .. | .. | .. | .. |
| **OECD ♦ | 97 164 | - 89 | 0 | - 100 | 30 031 | 147 | 69 463 | - 91 | 3 | - 100 | 26 882 | 156 | 0.08 | 0.03 | 0.11 |

♦ *See Technical Annex for data sources, notes and comments.*

**STATE AND TRENDS SUMMARY**

As a result of the Montreal Protocol, industrialised countries have rapidly decreased their production and consumption of CFCs (CFC 11, 12, 113, 114, 115) and halons (halon 1211, 1301 and 2402). Many countries achieved zero level by 1994 for halons and by end of 1995 for CFCs, HBFCs, carbon tetrachloride and methyl chloroform. As of 1996, there is no production or consumption (i.e. production + imports - exports) of these substances in industrialised countries except for certain essential uses, but there are still releases to the atmosphere. Efforts are being made to reduce international traffic (legal and illegal) in existing CFCs as well as intentional or accidental releases of existing CFCs. Imports and exports from non-Parties to the protocol are banned. Storage banks for existing halons and CFCs have been created in some countries. New measures have been adopted to phase out the supply of HCFCs and methyl bromide by 2020 and 2005 respectively in industrialised countries.

Global atmospheric concentrations of ODS show important changes. Growth rates of CFC concentrations have decreased since 1989, reflecting the impact of the Montreal Protocol and its amendments (page 18). Growth rates of HCFC concentrations are increasing. HCFCs have only 2 to 5 per cent of the ozone depleting potential of CFCs, but under current international agreements they will not be phased out for at least 20 years and will remain in the stratosphere for a long time. Stratospheric ozone depletion remains a source of concern due to the long time lag between the release of ODS and their arrival in the stratosphere.

## Total column ozone* over selected cities

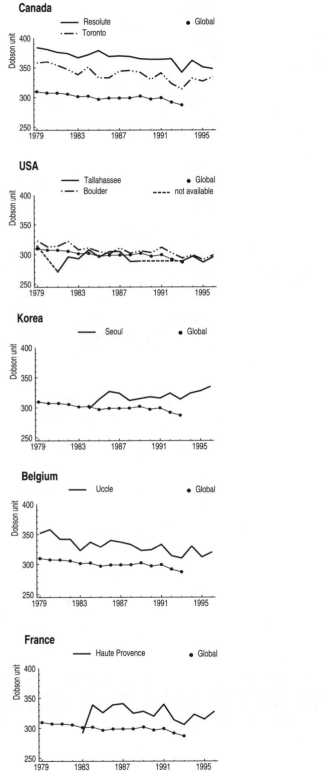

### Canada

Resolute ● Global
Toronto

### USA

Tallahassee ● Global
Boulder ---- not available

### Korea

Seoul ● Global

### Belgium

Uccle ● Global

### France

Haute Provence ● Global

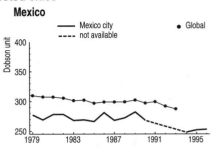

### Mexico

Mexico city ● Global
---- not available

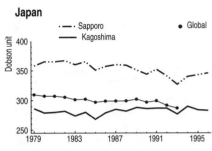

### Japan

Sapporo ● Global
Kagoshima

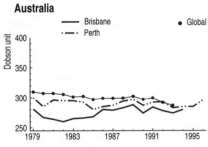

### Australia

Brisbane ● Global
Perth

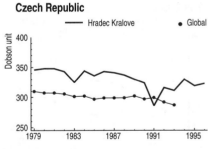

### Czech Republic

Hradec Kralove ● Global

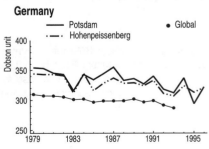

### Germany

Potsdam ● Global
Hohenpeissenberg

*OECD Environmental Indicators 1998*

## 4 STRATOSPHERIC OZONE

**Total column ozone\* over selected cities**

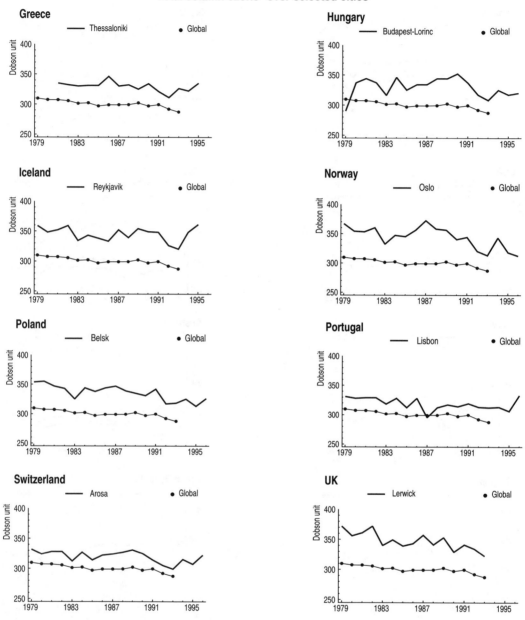

*\* See Technical Annex for further details.*

**STATE AND TRENDS
SUMMARY**

Since 1979, the amount of stratospheric ozone over the entire globe has decreased. The eruption of Mount Pinatubo in June 1991 caused levels to sink to record lows in 1992 and 1993. Trends also show a decrease in ozone levels over a number of cities. These trends, however, need continued monitoring and careful interpretation, due to possible interference with ground-level ozone.

# AIR QUALITY

*Atmospheric pollutants from energy transformation and energy consumption, but also from industrial processes, are the main contributors to regional and local air pollution. Major concerns relate to their effects on human health and ecosystems. Human exposure is particularly high in urban areas where economic activities are concentrated. Air pollution may also damage ecosystems, buildings and monuments, for example through acid precipitation and deposition.*

*Degraded air quality can result from and cause <u>unsustainable</u> development patterns. It can have substantial economic and social consequences, from medical costs and building restoration needs to reduced agricultural output, forest damage and a generally lower quality of life. <u>Performance</u> can be assessed against domestic objectives and international commitments. In Europe and North America, acidification has led to several international agreements. For example, under the Convention on Long-Range Transboundary Air Pollution (Geneva, 1979), protocols to reduce emissions of sulphur (Helsinki, 1985 and Oslo, 1994), nitrogen (Sofia, 1988) and VOCs (Geneva, 1991) have been adopted.*

*<u>Indicators</u> presented here relate to:*

♦ *<u>SO$_x$ and NO$_x$ emissions</u> and changes in them over time, as well as <u>emission intensities</u> expressed as quantities emitted per unit of GDP and per capita, presented with related changes in economic growth and fossil fuel supply. These indicators should be supplemented with information on the acidity of rain and snow in selected regions, and the exceedance of critical loads in soils and waters which reflect the actual acidification of the environment.*

♦ *<u>air quality</u> expressed as trends in annual <u>SO$_2$ and NO$_2$ concentrations</u> for selected cities. In the longer term, indicators should focus on population exposure to air pollution. They should be complemented with information on ground-level ozone and on other air pollutants.*

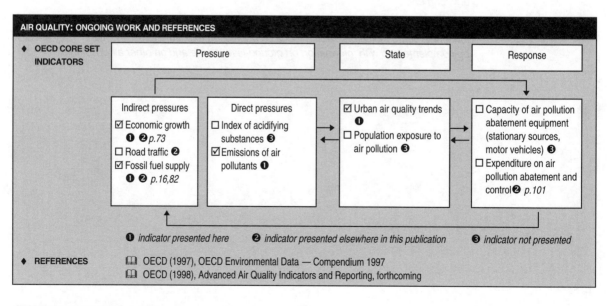

**AIR QUALITY: ONGOING WORK AND REFERENCES**

♦ **OECD CORE SET INDICATORS**

| Pressure | State | Response |
|---|---|---|

**Indirect pressures**
- ☑ Economic growth ❶ ❷ *p.73*
- ☐ Road traffic ❷
- ☑ Fossil fuel supply ❶ ❷ *p.16,82*

**Direct pressures**
- ☐ Index of acidifying substances ❸
- ☑ Emissions of air pollutants ❶

- ☑ Urban air quality trends ❶
- ☐ Population exposure to air pollution ❸

- ☐ Capacity of air pollution abatement equipment (stationary sources, motor vehicles) ❸
- ☐ Expenditure on air pollution abatement and control ❷ *p.101*

❶ *indicator presented here*  ❷ *indicator presented elsewhere in this publication*  ❸ *indicator not presented*

♦ **REFERENCES**
📖 OECD (1997), OECD Environmental Data — Compendium 1997
📖 OECD (1998), Advanced Air Quality Indicators and Reporting, forthcoming

## Sulphur oxide (SOx) emissions

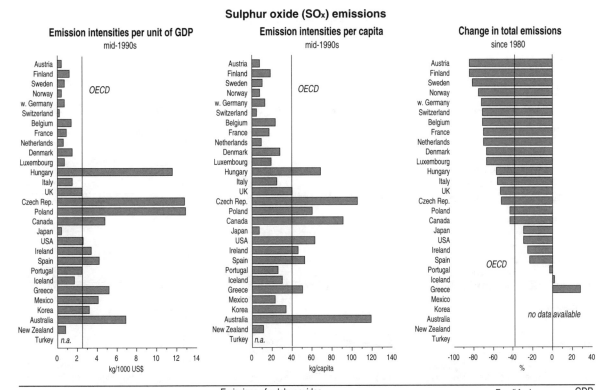

**Emission intensities per unit of GDP**
mid-1990s

**Emission intensities per capita**
mid-1990s

**Change in total emissions**
since 1980

| | | Emissions of sulphur oxides | | | | | | Fossil fuel supply | GDP |
|---|---|---|---|---|---|---|---|---|---|
| | | Total | | Intensities per unit of GDP | | Intensities per capita | | | |
| | | 1 000 t. mid-1990s | % change since 1980 | kg/1 000 US$ mid-1990s | % change since 1980 | kg/cap. mid-1990s | % change since 1980 | % change since 1980 | % change since 1980 |
| Canada | ♦ | 2668 | -43 | 4.8 | -59 | 91 | -52 | 12 | 43 |
| Mexico | | 2162 | .. | 4.1 | .. | 23 | .. | 28 | 29 |
| USA | ♦ | 16619 | -29 | 2.6 | -51 | 63 | -39 | 9 | 46 |
| Japan | ♦ | *903* | *-29* | *0.4* | *-54* | *7* | *-34* | 30 | 59 |
| Korea | ♦ | 1532 | .. | 3.2 | .. | 34 | .. | 199 | 241 |
| Australia | | 2150 | .. | 6.9 | .. | 119 | .. | 34 | 57 |
| New Zealand | | 41 | .. | 0.8 | .. | 11 | .. | 73 | 41 |
| Austria | ♦ | 64 | -84 | 0.4 | -88 | 8 | -85 | 10 | 37 |
| Belgium | | 240 | -71 | 1.4 | -77 | 24 | -72 | -4 | 28 |
| Czech Rep. | ♦ | 1091 | -52 | 12.8 | .. | 106 | -52 | -22 | .. |
| Denmark | ♦ | 148 | -67 | 1.5 | -75 | 28 | -68 | 3 | 35 |
| Finland | | 96 | -84 | 1.2 | -87 | 19 | -85 | -1 | 32 |
| France | | 1010 | -70 | 0.9 | -77 | 17 | -72 | -15 | 33 |
| Germany | ♦ | 2995 | .. | 2.1 | .. | 37 | .. | -13 | .. |
| w. Germany | | 874 | -72 | 0.7 | -79 | 13 | -74 | .. | 36 |
| Greece | ♦ | *510* | *28* | *5.2* | *9* | *51* | *22* | 49 | 24 |
| Hungary | ♦ | 705 | -57 | 11.6 | .. | 69 | -55 | -24 | .. |
| Iceland | ♦ | 8 | 2 | 1.7 | -19 | 30 | -10 | 22 | 36 |
| Ireland | ♦ | 166 | -25 | 3.4 | -55 | 46 | -29 | 35 | 84 |
| Italy | ♦ | *1424* | *-56* | *1.5* | *-65* | *25* | *-56* | 16 | 32 |
| Luxembourg | | 8 | -67 | 0.7 | -83 | 19 | -71 | -13 | 100 |
| Netherlands | ♦ | 148 | -70 | 0.6 | -78 | 10 | -72 | 11 | 38 |
| Norway | | 35 | -75 | 0.4 | -83 | 8 | -77 | 19 | 52 |
| Poland | | 2337 | -43 | 12.9 | .. | 61 | -47 | -20 | .. |
| Portugal | | 258 | -3 | 2.5 | -31 | 26 | -4 | 95 | 43 |
| Spain | ♦ | 2062 | -23 | 4.2 | -43 | 53 | -26 | 34 | 44 |
| Sweden | | 94 | -81 | 0.7 | -85 | 11 | -83 | -9 | 24 |
| Switzerland | | 33 | -71 | 0.2 | -77 | 5 | -74 | 8 | 23 |
| UK | ♦ | 2360 | -53 | 2.5 | -65 | 40 | -55 | 3 | 38 |
| OECD | ♦ | 43600 | -38 | 2.5 | .. | 40 | -45 | 10 | .. |

♦ *See Technical Annex for data sources, notes and comments.*

# 5 AIR EMISSION INTENSITIES

## Trends in SOx emissions, Index 1980 = 100

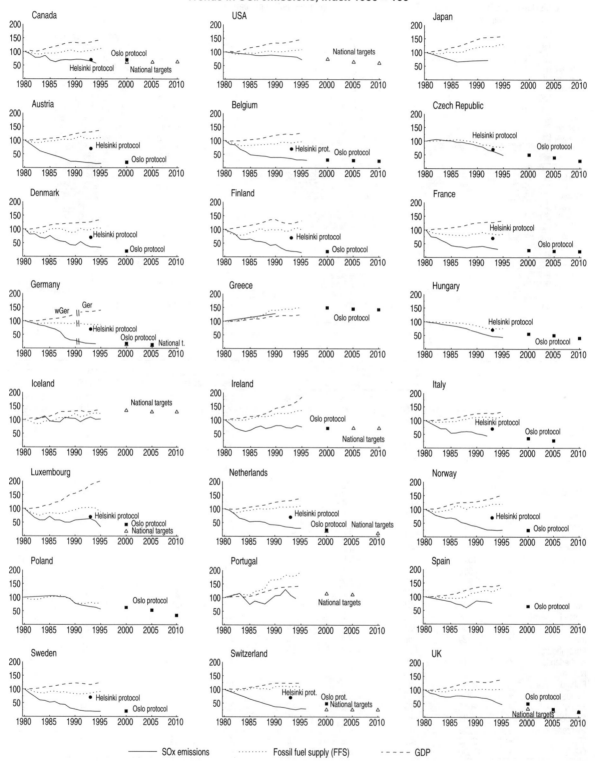

―――――― SOx emissions         ·········· Fossil fuel supply (FFS)         ― ― ― ― GDP

## AIR EMISSION INTENSITIES 5

### Nitrogen oxide (NOx) emissions

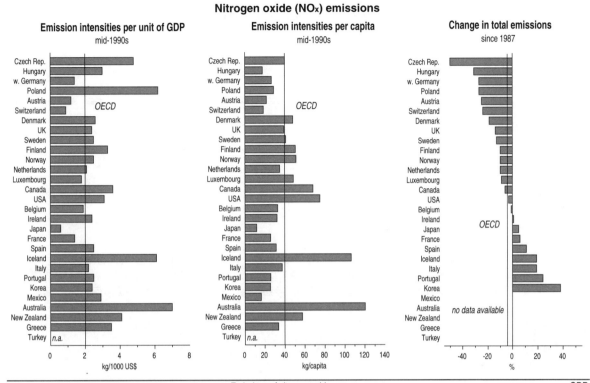

Emission intensities per unit of GDP
mid-1990s

Emission intensities per capita
mid-1990s

Change in total emissions
since 1987

| | | Emissions of nitrogen oxides | | | | | | Fossil fuel supply | GDP |
|---|---|---|---|---|---|---|---|---|---|---|
| | | Total | | | Intensities per unit of GDP | | Intensities per capita | | | |
| | | 1 000 t. mid-1990s | % change since 1980 | % change since 1987 | kg/1 000 US$ mid-1990s | % change since 1980 | kg/cap. mid-1990s | % change since 1980 | % change since 1980 | % change since 1980 |
| Canada | | 1995 | 2 | -6 | 4 | -27 | 68 | -14 | 12 | 43 |
| Mexico | | 1526 | .. | .. | 3 | .. | 16 | .. | 28 | 29 |
| USA | | 19758 | -6 | -3 | 3 | -35 | 75 | -19 | 9 | 46 |
| Japan | ◆ | *1455* | *-10* | *5* | *1* | *-42* | *12* | *-16* | 30 | 59 |
| Korea | ◆ | 1152 | .. | 38 | 2 | .. | 26 | .. | 199 | 241 |
| Australia | ◆ | 2174 | .. | .. | 7 | .. | 120 | .. | 34 | 57 |
| New Zealand | | 206 | .. | .. | 4 | .. | 58 | .. | 73 | 41 |
| Austria | ◆ | 175 | -29 | -25 | 1 | -47 | 22 | -33 | 10 | 37 |
| Belgium | | 334 | -24 | -1 | 2 | -40 | 33 | -27 | -4 | 28 |
| Czech Rep. | | 412 | -56 | -50 | 5 | .. | 40 | -56 | -22 | .. |
| Denmark | ◆ | 251 | -11 | -19 | 3 | -32 | 48 | -13 | 3 | 35 |
| Finland | | 258 | -13 | -10 | 3 | -31 | 51 | -18 | -1 | 32 |
| France | ◆ | 1494 | -9 | 6 | 1 | -30 | 26 | -16 | -15 | 33 |
| Germany | | 2210 | .. | .. | 2 | .. | 27 | .. | -13 | .. |
| w. Germany | | 1766 | -33 | -27 | 1 | -50 | 27 | -37 | .. | 36 |
| Greece | ◆ | *338* | *56* | .. | *3* | *33* | *34* | *49* | 49 | 24 |
| Hungary | | 182 | -33 | -31 | 3 | .. | 18 | -30 | -24 | .. |
| Iceland | ◆ | 28 | 34 | 19 | 6 | 6 | 106 | 17 | 22 | 36 |
| Ireland | ◆ | 116 | 40 | 1 | 2 | -16 | 32 | 33 | 35 | 84 |
| Italy | ◆ | *2117* | *34* | *19* | *2* | *5* | *37* | *33* | 16 | 32 |
| Luxembourg | ◆ | 20 | -13 | *-9* | 2 | -55 | 48 | -23 | -13 | 100 |
| Netherlands | ◆ | 540 | -8 | -10 | 2 | -31 | 35 | -15 | 11 | 38 |
| Norway | | 222 | 16 | -10 | 3 | -21 | 51 | 9 | 19 | 52 |
| Poland | | 1120 | -9 | -27 | 6 | .. | 29 | -16 | -20 | .. |
| Portugal | ◆ | 256 | 55 | 24 | 2 | 10 | 26 | 54 | 95 | 43 |
| Spain | ◆ | 1223 | 29 | *11* | 2 | -5 | 31 | 24 | 34 | 44 |
| Sweden | ◆ | 362 | -19 | *-13* | 3 | -33 | 41 | -24 | -9 | 24 |
| Switzerland | | 132 | -22 | -24 | 1 | -37 | 19 | -30 | 8 | 23 |
| UK | | *2293* | -5 | -14 | *2* | -29 | *39* | -9 | 3 | 38 |
| OECD | ◆ | 42900 | -3 | -4 | 2 | .. | 40 | -14 | 10 | .. |

◆ *See Technical Annex for data sources, notes and comments.*

# 5 AIR EMISSION INTENSITIES

## Trends in NOx emissions, Index 1980 = 100

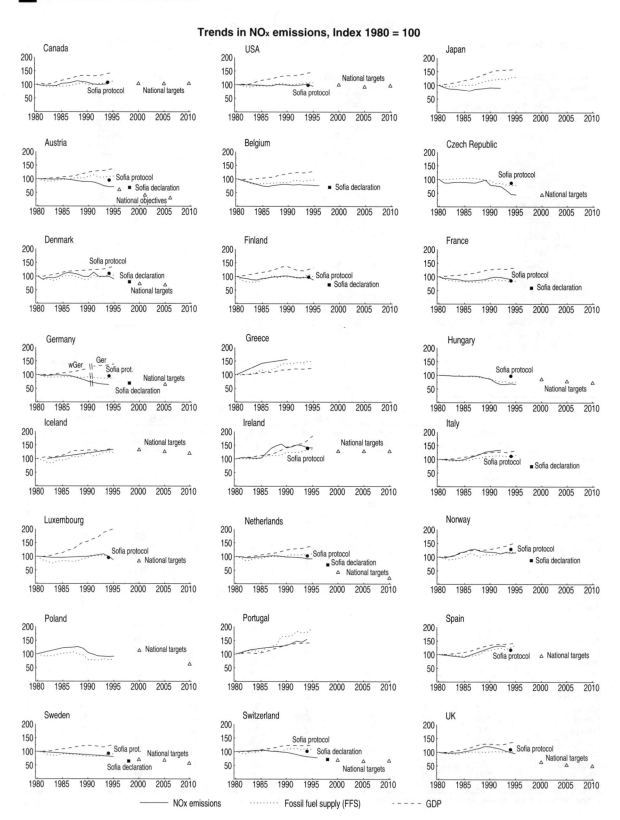

NOx emissions ········· Fossil fuel supply (FFS) - - - - GDP

**STATE AND TRENDS**
**SUMMARY**

$SO_x$ emission intensities per capita and per unit of GDP show significant variations among OECD countries. A *clear decoupling* of emissions from GDP is seen in many countries.

Emissions have decreased significantly for the OECD as a whole, compared to 1980 levels, as a combined result of:

♦ structural changes in the economy;

♦ changes in energy demand through energy savings and fuel substitution;

♦ pollution control policies and technical progress, including countries' efforts to control large stationary emission sources.

$NO_x$ emissions have decreased in the OECD overall compared to 1980, but less than $SO_x$ emissions. Major progress in the early 1990s, particularly in some European countries, reflects changes in energy demand, pollution control policies and technical progress. However, these results have not compensated in all countries for steady growth in road traffic, fossil fuel use and other activities generating $NO_x$.

Emission intensities per capita and per unit of GDP show significant variations among OECD countries, and a weak decoupling of emissions from GDP in a number of countries.

# 6 URBAN AIR QUALITY

## Trends in SO₂ concentrations in selected cities, Index 1990 = 100

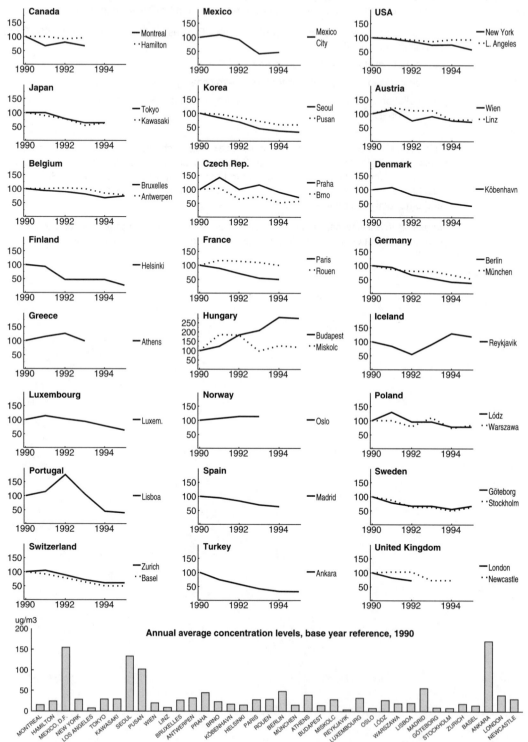

ug/m3

**Annual average concentration levels, base year reference, 1990**

## Trends in NO₂ concentrations in selected cities, Index 1990 = 100

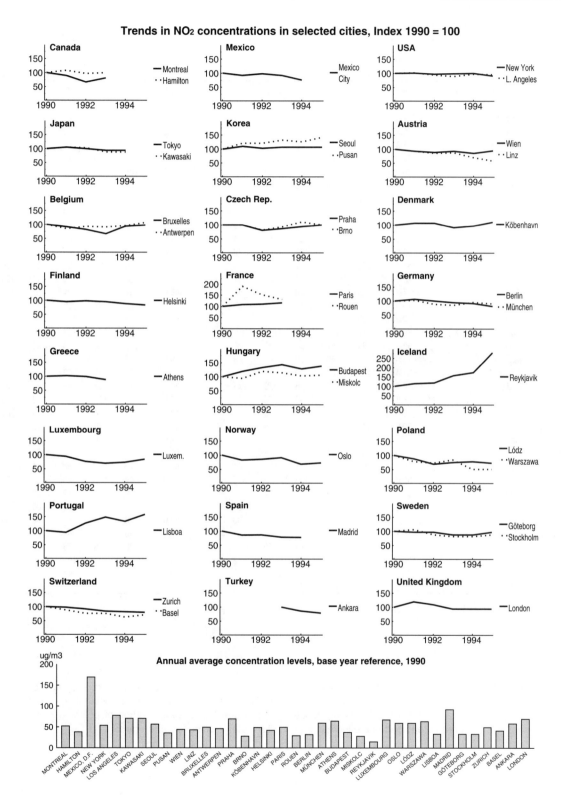

ug/m3

**Annual average concentration levels, base year reference, 1990**

## 6 URBAN AIR QUALITY

| | | | Annual concentrations of sulphur dioxide | | | | | | | Annual concentrations of nitrogen dioxide | | | | | | |
|---|---|---|---|---|---|---|---|---|---|---|---|---|---|---|---|---|
| | | | base reference (µg/m3) | (Index 1990 = 100) | | | | | | base reference (µg/m3) | (Index 1990 = 100) | | | | | |
| | | | 1990 | 1991 | 1992 | 1993 | 1994 | 1995 | | 1990 | 1991 | 1992 | 1993 | 1994 | 1995 |
| Canada | Montreal | ♦ | 15.0 | 67 | 80 | 67 | .. | .. | | 52.0 | 90 | 67 | 81 | .. | .. |
| | Hamilton | ♦ | 24.0 | 100 | 92 | 96 | .. | .. | | 38.0 | 108 | 97 | 100 | .. | .. |
| Mexico | Mexico, D.F. | | 154.5 | 109 | 92 | 41 | 47 | .. | | 169.2 | 92 | 98 | 92 | 76 | .. |
| USA | New York | | 28.4 | 96 | 86 | 74 | 75 | 57 | | 53.6 | 101 | 97 | 99 | 100 | 91 |
| | Los Angeles | | 7.3 | 99 | 92 | 86 | 93 | 93 | | 77.5 | 102 | 94 | 89 | 97 | 96 |
| Japan | Tokyo | ♦ | 29.0 | 100 | 79 | 64 | 64 | .. | | 70.1 | 105 | 100 | 94 | 94 | .. |
| | Kawasaki | ♦ | 29.1 | 89 | 79 | 54 | 63 | .. | | 70.1 | 105 | 103 | 88 | 88 | .. |
| Korea | Seoul | | 133.6 | 84 | 69 | 45 | 37 | 33 | | 56.4 | 110 | 103 | 107 | 107 | 107 |
| | Pusan | | 102.2 | 97 | 85 | 72 | 59 | 59 | | 35.7 | 121 | 121 | 132 | 126 | 142 |
| Austria | Wien | | 20.0 | 115 | 75 | 90 | 75 | 70 | | 44.0 | 93 | 89 | 93 | 86 | 95 |
| | Linz | | 9.0 | 122 | 111 | 111 | 78 | 78 | | 43.0 | 93 | 86 | 88 | 70 | 58 |
| Belgium | Bruxelles | | 27.0 | 93 | 89 | 81 | 67 | 74 | | 49.0 | 92 | 82 | 67 | 94 | 98 |
| | Antwerpen | | 32.0 | 100 | 103 | 100 | 84 | 78 | | 46.0 | 85 | 93 | 91 | 96 | 107 |
| Czech Rep. | Praha | | 45.0 | 142 | 100 | 116 | 89 | 71 | | 69.0 | 100 | 81 | 87 | 94 | 100 |
| | Brno | | 23.0 | 104 | 65 | 74 | 52 | 57 | | 28.0 | 100 | 82 | 93 | 111 | 100 |
| Denmark | Köbenhavn | | 17.2 | 108 | 81 | 70 | 51 | 42 | | 48.6 | 107 | 107 | 91 | 97 | 111 |
| Finland | Helsinki | ♦ | 15.0 | 93 | 47 | 47 | 47 | 27 | | 42.0 | 95 | 98 | 95 | 88 | 83 |
| France | Paris | ♦ | 28.0 | 89 | 71 | 54 | 50 | .. | | 49.0 | 108 | 110 | 116 | .. | .. |
| | Rouen | ♦ | 29.0 | 117 | 114 | 110 | 100 | .. | | 29.0 | 190 | 152 | 131 | .. | .. |
| Germany | Berlin | | 48.0 | 94 | 67 | 54 | 42 | 38 | | 32.0 | 106 | 100 | 94 | 91 | 81 |
| | München | | 15.0 | 87 | 80 | 80 | 67 | 53 | | 59.0 | 102 | 88 | 85 | 95 | 90 |
| Greece | Athens | | 39.4 | 115 | 126 | 99 | .. | .. | | 63.9 | 102 | 99 | 88 | .. | .. |
| Hungary | Budapest | | 14.1 | 123 | 184 | 208 | 279 | 274 | | 37.0 | 119 | 133 | 143 | 128 | 138 |
| | Miskolc | | 28.5 | 186 | 183 | 98 | 126 | 119 | | 28.0 | 94 | 119 | 114 | 103 | 106 |
| Iceland | Reykjavik | ♦ | 3.8 | 84 | 55 | 90 | 129 | 118 | | 14.8 | 114 | 118 | 157 | 174 | 281 |
| Luxembourg | Luxembourg | ♦ | 32.0 | 114 | 103 | 94 | 78 | 63 | | 67.0 | 94 | 76 | 70 | 73 | 84 |
| Norway | Oslo | ♦ | 7.3 | 107 | 114 | 114 | .. | .. | | 59.0 | 83 | 86 | 91 | 68 | 73 |
| Poland | Lódz | | 27.0 | 130 | 96 | 96 | 78 | 78 | | 59.0 | 88 | 69 | 75 | 78 | 73 |
| | Warszawa | | 19.0 | 100 | 79 | 111 | 74 | 84 | | 63.0 | 78 | 73 | 84 | 51 | 51 |
| Portugal | Lisboa | ♦ | 20.0 | 115 | 175 | 105 | 45 | 40 | | 33.0 | 94 | 127 | 148 | 133 | 158 |
| Spain | Madrid | ♦ | 56.0 | 95 | 84 | 70 | 64 | .. | | 92.0 | 86 | 87 | 79 | 78 | .. |
| Sweden | Göteborg | ♦ | 9.0 | 78 | 67 | 67 | 56 | 67 | | 33.0 | 97 | 97 | 88 | 88 | 97 |
| | Stockholm | ♦ | 8.0 | 88 | 63 | 63 | 50 | 63 | | 33.0 | 106 | 88 | 82 | 82 | 88 |
| Switzerland | Zurich | | 18.1 | 105 | 89 | 72 | 61 | 61 | | 49.0 | 98 | 92 | 84 | 82 | 80 |
| | Basel | | 14.1 | 92 | 78 | 64 | 50 | 50 | | 41.0 | 88 | 76 | 76 | 63 | 71 |
| Turkey | Ankara | ♦ | 170.0 | 74 | .. | 42 | 33 | 32 | | 58.0 | .. | .. | 100 | 86 | 79 |
| UK | London | ♦ | 39.0 | 82 | 72 | .. | .. | .. | | 69.0 | 119 | 109 | 94 | 94 | 94 |
| | Newcastle | ♦ | 30.0 | 103 | 103 | 73 | 73 | .. | | .. | .. | .. | .. | .. | .. |

♦ *See Technical Annex for data sources, notes and comments.*

**STATE AND TRENDS SUMMARY**

Urban air quality has slowly continued to improve, particularly with respect to $SO_2$ concentrations; but ground-level ozone, $NO_2$ concentrations, toxic air pollutants and related health effects raise growing concern, largely due to the concentration of pollution sources in urban areas and to the increasing use of private vehicles for urban trips.

# WASTE

*Waste is generated at all stages of human activities. Its composition and amounts depend largely on consumption and production patterns. Main concerns relate to the potential impact on human health and the environment (soil, water, air and landscape). Hazardous waste, mainly from industry, is of particular concern since it entails serious environmental risks if badly managed. Also, long-term policies are needed for the disposal of high-level radioactive waste.*

*Waste management issues are at environmental centre stage in many countries. Responses have been directed mainly towards collection, treatment and disposal. Increasingly, waste minimisation is an aim of <u>sustainable development strategies</u>. It can be achieved through waste prevention, reuse, recycling and recovery, and more broadly through better integration of environmental concerns in consumption and production patterns. <u>Performance</u> can be assessed against domestic objectives and international commitments. Agreements and regulations on waste in general and transfrontier movements of hazardous waste in particular include directives of the European Union, OECD Decisions and Recommendations, the Lomé IV Convention and the 1989 Basel Convention.*

*<u>Indicators</u> presented here relate to:*

♦ *<u>waste generation</u>, i.e.:*

– *total amounts of waste by principal source sector (municipal, industrial and nuclear waste), as well as <u>generation intensities</u> expressed per capita and per unit of GDP. Treatment and disposal shares of municipal waste are shown as complementary information.*

– *hazardous waste produced per unit of GDP (hazardous waste generation is largely driven by production patterns). This indicator does not reflect toxicity levels or other risks posed by such waste, nor its real impact on the environment. Transfrontier movements are shown as complementary information.*

*Indicators of waste generation intensity are first approximations of potential environmental pressure; more information is needed to describe the actual pressure.*

♦ *<u>waste recycling</u> rates for paper and glass. They present total amounts recycled as percentage of the apparent consumption of the respective material.*

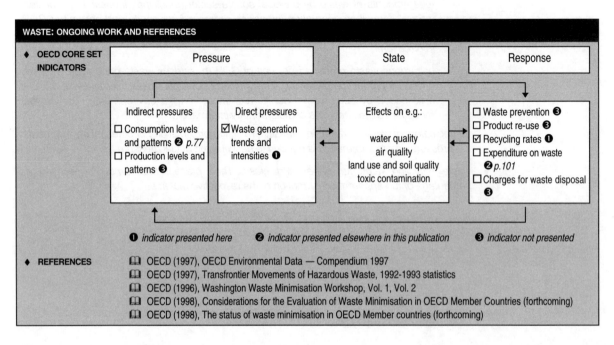

**WASTE: ONGOING WORK AND REFERENCES**

| ◆ OECD CORE SET INDICATORS | Pressure | State | Response |
|---|---|---|---|

| Indirect pressures | Direct pressures | Effects on e.g.: | ☐ Waste prevention ❸ |
|---|---|---|---|
| ☐ Consumption levels and patterns ❷ *p.77* <br> ☐ Production levels and patterns ❸ | ☑ Waste generation trends and intensities ❶ | water quality <br> air quality <br> land use and soil quality <br> toxic contamination | ☐ Product re-use ❸ <br> ☑ Recycling rates ❶ <br> ☐ Expenditure on waste ❷ *p.101* <br> ☐ Charges for waste disposal ❸ |

❶ *indicator presented here*    ❷ *indicator presented elsewhere in this publication*    ❸ *indicator not presented*

◆ **REFERENCES**    📖 OECD (1997), OECD Environmental Data — Compendium 1997
📖 OECD (1997), Transfrontier Movements of Hazardous Waste, 1992-1993 statistics
📖 OECD (1996), Washington Waste Minimisation Workshop, Vol. 1, Vol. 2
📖 OECD (1998), Considerations for the Evaluation of Waste Minimisation in OECD Member Countries (forthcoming)
📖 OECD (1998), The status of waste minimisation in OECD Member countries (forthcoming)

## WASTE GENERATION  7

### Municipal waste, state

**Generation intensities per capita**

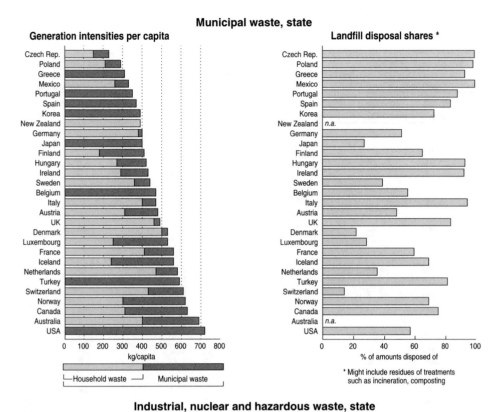

kg/capita

└─Household waste ─┘ Municipal waste

**Landfill disposal shares ***

% of amounts disposed of

* Might include residues of treatments
such as incineration, composting

### Industrial, nuclear and hazardous waste, state

**Industrial waste per unit of GDP**     **Nuclear waste per capita**     **Hazardous waste per unit of GDP**

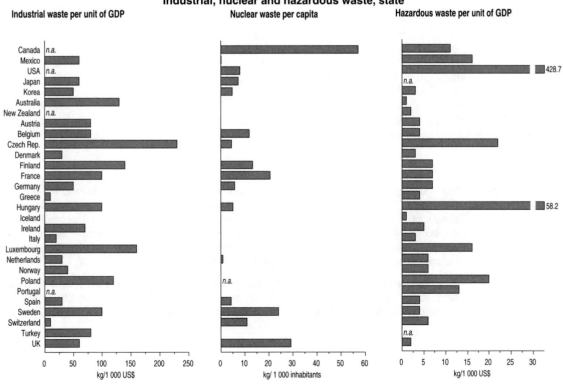

kg/1 000 US$     kg/ 1 000 inhabitants     kg/1 000 US$

*OECD Environmental Indicators 1998*

## 7 WASTE GENERATION

### Municipal waste

| | | Municipal waste generated per capita | | *of which:* Household waste | Private final consumption expenditure, per capita | | Management of municipal waste % of amounts disposed of | | |
|---|---|---|---|---|---|---|---|---|---|
| | | kg/cap. mid-1990s | % change since 1980 | kg/cap. mid-1990s | 1 000 US$/cap. 1995 | % change since 1980 | Recycling/ compost. mid-1990s | Incineration mid-1990s | Landfill mid-1990s |
| Canada | ♦ | 630 | 24 | 310 | 11.0 | 18.3 | 19 | 6 | 75 |
| Mexico | ♦ | 330 | .. | 260 | 3.5 | -7.1 | 1 | - | 99 |
| USA | ♦ | 720 | 19 | .. | 16.8 | 31.6 | 27 | 16 | 57 |
| Japan | ♦ | 400 | 7 | .. | 11.0 | 47.5 | 4 | 69 | 27 |
| Korea | ♦ | 390 | .. | .. | 6.3 | 164.9 | 24 | 4 | 72 |
| Australia | ♦ | 690 | .. | 400 | 10.4 | 29.3 | .. | .. | .. |
| New Zealand | ♦ | .. | .. | 390 | 8.9 | 18.3 | .. | .. | .. |
| Austria | ♦ | 480 | *42* | 310 | 10.1 | 32.3 | 38 | 14 | 48 |
| Belgium | ♦ | 470 | .. | .. | 11.0 | 21.7 | 14 | 31 | 55 |
| Czech Rep. | ♦ | 230 | .. | 150 | 5.1 | .. | - | - | 99 |
| Denmark | ♦ | 530 | 34 | 500 | 9.7 | 27.4 | 23 | 54 | 22 |
| Finland | ♦ | 410 | .. | 180 | 7.5 | 21.6 | 33 | 2 | 65 |
| France | ♦ | 560 | *8* | 410 | 10.7 | 23.5 | 9 | 32 | 59 |
| Germany | ♦ | 400 | .. | 380 | 10.4 | *27.5* | 29 | 17 | 51 |
| Greece | ♦ | 310 | *20* | .. | 7.4 | 28.4 | 7 | - | 93 |
| Hungary | ♦ | 420 | 82 | 270 | 4.0 | .. | - | 7 | 93 |
| Iceland | ♦ | 560 | .. | 240 | 9.7 | 13.0 | 14 | 17 | 69 |
| Ireland | ♦ | 430 | 129 | 290 | 8.3 | 40.1 | 8 | .. | 92 |
| Italy | ♦ | 470 | 89 | 400 | 11.1 | 33.5 | .. | 6 | 94 |
| Luxembourg | ♦ | 530 | 51 | 250 | 16.5 | 36.3 | 28 | 43 | 28 |
| Netherlands | ♦ | 580 | 16 | 470 | 10.5 | 18.6 | 38 | 27 | 35 |
| Norway | ♦ | 620 | 49 | 300 | 9.2 | 30.2 | 15 | 16 | 69 |
| Poland | ♦ | 290 | 10 | 210 | 2.9 | .. | 2 | - | 98 |
| Portugal | ♦ | 350 | 75 | .. | 6.8 | 43.9 | 12 | - | 88 |
| Spain | ♦ | 370 | 35 | .. | 7.8 | 28.8 | 12 | 4 | 83 |
| Sweden | ♦ | 440 | 21 | 360 | 8.3 | 7.5 | 19 | 42 | 39 |
| Switzerland | ♦ | 610 | *32* | 430 | 12.0 | 8.2 | 40 | 46 | 14 |
| Turkey | ♦ | 590 | 44 | .. | 3.3 | 12.5 | 2 | 2 | 81 |
| UK | ♦ | 490 | .. | 460 | 10.6 | 41.5 | 7 | 9 | 83 |
| * **OECD | ♦ | 530 | 25 | .. | 11.4 | 38.3 | .. | .. | .. |

♦ *See Technical Annex for data sources, notes and comments.*

**STATE AND TRENDS**
**SUMMARY**

The quantity of municipal waste generated has steadily increased in recent decades. Generation intensity per capita has risen from 1980, mostly in line with private final consumption expenditure and GDP. In some countries growth rates even exceeded those of the economy. The amount and composition of municipal waste vary widely among OECD countries, being directly related to levels and patterns of consumption and also depending on national waste management and minimisation practices.

In a number of OECD countries, incineration and recycling are increasingly used to reduce amounts of waste going to final disposal, and particularly to landfill. Landfill nonetheless remains the major disposal method in most OECD countries.

## WASTE GENERATION 7

### Industrial, nuclear and hazardous waste

| | | Industrial waste | | Nuclear waste | | Hazardous waste | | | | |
| --- | --- | --- | --- | --- | --- | --- | --- | --- | --- | --- |
| | | Waste from the manuf. industry, mid-1990s | | Spent fuel arisings, 1995 | | Production | | | Net transfrontier movements | Amounts to be managed |
| | | Total 1 000 tonnes | per unit of GDP kg/ 1 000 US$ | Total tonnes HM | per capita kg/ 1 000 inh. | Year | Total 1 000 tonnes | per unit of GDP kg/ 1 000 US$ | Exports-Imports 1 000 tonnes | 1 000 tonnes |
| Canada | | .. | .. | 1 690 | 57.1 | 1991 | 5 896 | 11.3 | 87.9 | 5 808 |
| Mexico | ◆ | 29570 | 60 | 20 | 0.2 | 1995 | 8 000 | 16.1 | - 152.8 | 8 153 |
| USA | ◆ | .. | .. | 2 100 | 8.0 | 1993 | 213 620 | 428.7 | 142.7 | 191 091 |
| Japan | ◆ | 143710 | 60 | 914 | 7.3 | 1995 | .. | .. | 2.0 | .. |
| Korea | ◆ | 27010 | 50 | 216 | 4.8 | 1995 | 1 622 | 3.1 | - | 1 622 |
| Australia | ◆ | 37040 | 130 | - | - | 1992 | 426 | 1.5 | 3.0 | 423 |
| New Zealand | ◆ | .. | .. | - | - | 1993 | 110 | 2.3 | 10.5 | 100 |
| Austria | ◆ | 10470 | 80 | - | - | 1994 | 513 | 3.6 | 10.9 | 502 |
| Belgium | ◆ | 13370 | 80 | 121 | 11.9 | 1994 | 776 | 4.4 | - 317.0 | 1 093 |
| Czech Rep. | ◆ | 19770 | 230 | 46 | 4.5 | 1994 | 1 867 | 21.9 | - 4.9 | 1 872 |
| Denmark | ◆ | 2560 | 30 | - | - | 1995 | 250 | 2.6 | - 34.0 | 284 |
| Finland | ◆ | 11400 | 140 | 68 | 13.3 | 1992 | 559 | 7.5 | 16.6 | 542 |
| France | ◆ | 105000 | 100 | 1 200 | 20.6 | 1990 | 7 000 | 6.8 | - 447.6 | .. |
| Germany | ◆ | 64860 | 50 | 470 | 5.8 | 1993 | 9 100 | 6.6 | 522.6 | 8 577 |
| Greece | ◆ | 510 | 10 | - | - | 1992 | 450 | 4.5 | 0.1 | 450 |
| Hungary | ◆ | 6330 | 100 | 52 | 5.1 | 1994 | 3 537 | 58.2 | 9.6 | 3 527 |
| Iceland | ◆ | 10 | - | - | - | 1994 | 6 | 1.3 | 0.8 | 5 |
| Ireland | ◆ | 3780 | 70 | - | - | 1995 | 248 | 4.6 | 16.4 | 231 |
| Italy | ◆ | 22210 | 20 | - | - | 1991 | 3 387 | 3.5 | 13.0 | 3 374 |
| Luxembourg | ◆ | 1440 | 160 | - | - | 1995 | 180 | 15.7 | 180.0 | - |
| Netherlands | ◆ | 7920 | 30 | 14 | 0.9 | 1993 | 1 520 | 6.0 | - 73.5 | 1 593 |
| Norway | ◆ | 3290 | 40 | - | - | 1994 | 500 | 5.7 | 28.4 | 472 |
| Poland | ◆ | 22610 | 120 | .. | .. | 1995 | 3 866 | 20.0 | .. | .. |
| Portugal | | .. | .. | - | - | 1994 | 1 356 | 13.2 | - 6.2 | 1 363 |
| Spain | ◆ | 13830 | 30 | 168 | 4.3 | 1987 | 1 708 | 4.0 | - 75.0 | 1 783 |
| Sweden | ◆ | 13970 | 100 | 213 | 24.1 | 1985 | 500 | 3.8 | 30.0 | 470 |
| Switzerland | ◆ | 1350 | 10 | 77 | 10.9 | 1995 | 834 | 5.6 | 96.0 | 738 |
| Turkey | ◆ | 25040 | 80 | - | - | .. | .. | .. | .. | .. |
| UK | ◆ | 56000 | 60 | 1 713 | 29.2 | 93/94 | 1 844 | 1.9 | - 68.0 | 1 912 |
| OECD | ◆ | 1500000 | 90 | 9 082 | 8.4 | .. | .. | .. | .. | .. |

◆ *See Technical Annex for data sources, notes and comments.*

**STATE AND TRENDS SUMMARY**

Industry has been generating increasing amounts of waste in recent decades. Changes in production patterns and related technologies, and in waste management practices, have altered the composition of such waste.

Generation intensities per unit of GDP reflect wide variations among OECD countries, in particular for hazardous waste.

Nuclear waste is directly related to the share of nuclear power in national energy supply and the types of nuclear technology adopted.

## 8 WASTE RECYCLING

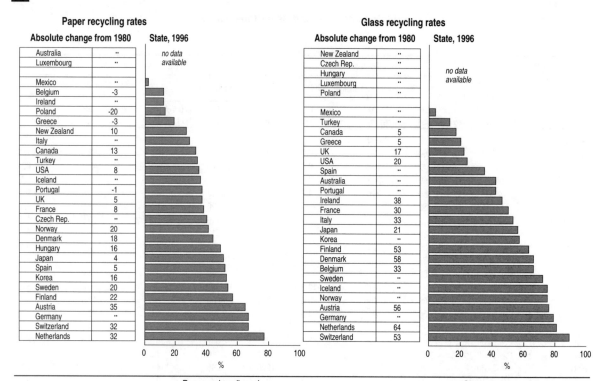

| Paper recycling rates |  |
| :--- | :--- |
| **Absolute change from 1980** | **State, 1996** |

| | |
| :--- | :--- |
| Australia | .. |
| Luxembourg | .. |
| | |
| Mexico | .. |
| Belgium | -3 |
| Ireland | .. |
| Poland | -20 |
| Greece | -3 |
| New Zealand | 10 |
| Italy | .. |
| Canada | 13 |
| Turkey | .. |
| USA | 8 |
| Iceland | .. |
| Portugal | -1 |
| UK | 5 |
| France | 8 |
| Czech Rep. | .. |
| Norway | 20 |
| Denmark | 18 |
| Hungary | 16 |
| Japan | 4 |
| Spain | 5 |
| Korea | 16 |
| Sweden | 20 |
| Finland | 22 |
| Austria | 35 |
| Germany | .. |
| Switzerland | 32 |
| Netherlands | 32 |

| Glass recycling rates |  |
| :--- | :--- |
| **Absolute change from 1980** | **State, 1996** |

| | |
| :--- | :--- |
| New Zealand | .. |
| Czech Rep. | .. |
| Hungary | .. |
| Luxembourg | .. |
| Poland | .. |
| | |
| Mexico | .. |
| Turkey | .. |
| Canada | 5 |
| Greece | 5 |
| UK | 17 |
| USA | 20 |
| Spain | .. |
| Australia | .. |
| Portugal | .. |
| Ireland | 38 |
| France | 30 |
| Italy | 33 |
| Japan | 21 |
| Korea | .. |
| Finland | 53 |
| Denmark | 58 |
| Belgium | 33 |
| Sweden | .. |
| Iceland | .. |
| Norway | .. |
| Austria | 56 |
| Germany | .. |
| Netherlands | 64 |
| Switzerland | 53 |

|  | Paper and cardboard | | | | | | Glass | | | | |
| :--- | :--- | :--- | :--- | :--- | :--- | :--- | :--- | :--- | :--- | :--- | :--- |
|  | Recycling rate, % | | | | Absolute change | | Recycling rate, % | | | | Absolute change |
|  | 1980 | 1985 | 1990 | 1996 | since 1980 | | 1980 | 1985 | 1990 | 1996 | since 1980 |
| Canada | 20 | 23 | 28 | 33 | 13 | ♦ | 12 | 12 | .. | 17 | 5 |
| Mexico ♦ | .. | .. | 2 | 2 | .. | ♦ | .. | .. | 4 | 4 | .. |
| USA | 27 | 27 | 34 | 35 | 8 | ♦ | 5 | 8 | 20 | 24 | 20 |
| Japan | 48 | 50 | 50 | 51 | 4 | ♦ | 35 | 47 | 48 | 56 | 21 |
| Korea | 37 | .. | 44 | 53 | 16 | | .. | .. | 46 | 57 | .. |
| Australia ♦ | .. | 36 | 51 | .. | .. | | .. | .. | .. | 42 | .. |
| New Zealand | 17 | 19 | 20 | 27 | 10 | | .. | .. | .. | .. | .. |
| Austria | 30 | 37 | 37 | 65 | 35 | | 20 | 38 | 60 | 76 | 56 |
| Belgium ♦ | 15 | 14 | .. | 12 | -3 | | 33 | 42 | 55 | 66 | 33 |
| Czech Rep. | .. | .. | .. | 40 | .. | | .. | .. | .. | .. | .. |
| Denmark | 26 | 31 | 35 | 44 | 18 | | 8 | 19 | 35 | 66 | 58 |
| Finland | 35 | 39 | 41 | 57 | 22 | | 10 | 21 | 36 | 63 | 53 |
| France | 30 | 35 | 34 | 38 | 8 | | 20 | 26 | 29 | 50 | 30 |
| Germany ♦ | *34* | *43* | *44* | 67 | .. | ♦ | *23* | *43* | *54* | 79 | .. |
| Greece ♦ | 22 | 25 | 28 | 19 | -3 | ♦ | 15 | 15 | 15 | 20 | 5 |
| Hungary | 33 | 42 | 53 | 49 | 16 | | .. | .. | .. | .. | .. |
| Iceland | .. | .. | .. | 36 | .. | | .. | .. | 70 | 75 | .. |
| Ireland | .. | 10 | .. | 12 | .. | | 8 | 7 | 23 | 46 | 38 |
| Italy | .. | 25 | 27 | 29 | .. | ♦ | 20 | 25 | 48 | 53 | 33 |
| Luxembourg | .. | .. | .. | .. | .. | | .. | .. | .. | .. | .. |
| Netherlands ♦ | 46 | 50 | 50 | 77 | 32 | ♦ | 17 | 49 | 67 | 81 | 64 |
| Norway ♦ | 22 | 21 | 25 | 41 | 20 | ♦ | .. | .. | 22 | 75 | .. |
| Poland | *34* | *34* | *46* | *13* | -20 | | .. | .. | .. | .. | .. |
| Portugal | 38 | 37 | 41 | 37 | -1 | | .. | 10 | 27 | 42 | .. |
| Spain | 47 | 57 | 51 | 52 | 5 | ♦ | .. | 13 | 27 | 35 | .. |
| Sweden | 34 | .. | 43 | 54 | 20 | | .. | 20 | 44 | 72 | .. |
| Switzerland | 35 | 39 | 49 | 67 | 32 | | 36 | 46 | 65 | 89 | 53 |
| Turkey | .. | .. | 27 | 34 | .. | | .. | 33 | 31 | 13 | .. |
| UK | 32 | 29 | 35 | 37 | 5 | ♦ | 5 | 12 | 21 | 22 | 17 |

♦ *See Technical Annex for data sources, notes and comments.*

**STATE AND TRENDS SUMMARY**

Recycling of glass and paper is increasing in most OECD countries as a result of evolving consumption patterns and waste management and minimisation practices.

# WATER QUALITY

*Water quality, closely linked to water quantity, is of <u>economic, environmental and social importance</u>.  A complex concept with many aspects (physical, chemical, microbial, biological), it can be defined in terms of a water body's suitability for various uses, such as water supply source, swimming or protection of aquatic life.  It is affected by water abstractions, by pollution loads from human activities (agriculture, industry, households), and by climate and weather.*

*If pressure from human activities becomes so intense that water quality is impaired to the point that drinking water requires ever more advanced and costly treatment or that aquatic plant and animal species in rivers and lakes are greatly reduced, then the <u>sustainability</u> of water resource use is in question.  <u>Performance</u> can be assessed against domestic objectives and international commitments.  At national level, countries have set receiving water standards, effluent limits and pollution load reduction targets for a range of parameters (e.g. oxygen, nutrients, micropollutants).  In many cases, they are also committed to international agreements such as the Oslo and Paris Conventions on the Prevention of Marine Pollution, the International Joint Commission Agreement on Great Lakes Water Quality in North America or the EU water directives.  Protection of freshwater quality and supply is an important part of Agenda 21, adopted at UNCED (Rio de Janeiro, 1992).*

*<u>Indicators</u> presented here relate to:*

♦   *<u>river water quality</u>, presenting two parameters (oxygen and nitrate content) for selected rivers. Data are shown for representative sites at the mouth or downstream frontier, giving a summary view of the pollution load and clean-up efforts on the upstream watershed.*

♦   *<u>waste water treatment</u>, particularly sewage treatment connection rates, i.e. the percentage of the national resident population actually served by public waste water treatment plants.  The extent of secondary and/or tertiary (chemical and/or biological) sewage treatment provides an indication of efforts to reduce pollution loads.  It does not take into account private facilities, used where public systems are not economic.  This indicator should be related to an optimal national connection rate taking into account national specificities such as population in remote areas.  Sewerage connection rates and public expenditure on waste water treatment are given as supplementary information.*

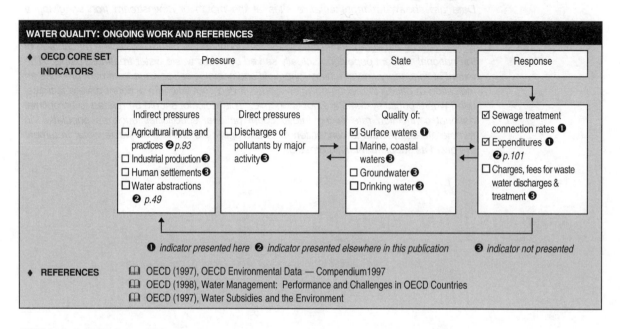

**WATER QUALITY: ONGOING WORK AND REFERENCES**

◆ **OECD CORE SET INDICATORS**

| Pressure | State | Response |
|---|---|---|

| Indirect pressures | Direct pressures | Quality of: | |
|---|---|---|---|
| ☐ Agricultural inputs and practices ❷ *p.93*<br>☐ Industrial production ❸<br>☐ Human settlements ❸<br>☐ Water abstractions ❷ *p.49* | ☐ Discharges of pollutants by major activity ❸ | ☑ Surface waters ❶<br>☐ Marine, coastal waters ❸<br>☐ Groundwater ❸<br>☐ Drinking water ❸ | ☑ Sewage treatment connection rates ❶<br>☑ Expenditures ❶ ❷ *p.101*<br>☐ Charges, fees for waste water discharges & treatment ❸ |

❶ *indicator presented here* ❷ *indicator presented elsewhere in this publication* ❸ *indicator not presented*

◆ **REFERENCES**   📖 OECD (1997), OECD Environmental Data — Compendium 1997
📖 OECD (1998), Water Management: Performance and Challenges in OECD Countries
📖 OECD (1997), Water Subsidies and the Environment

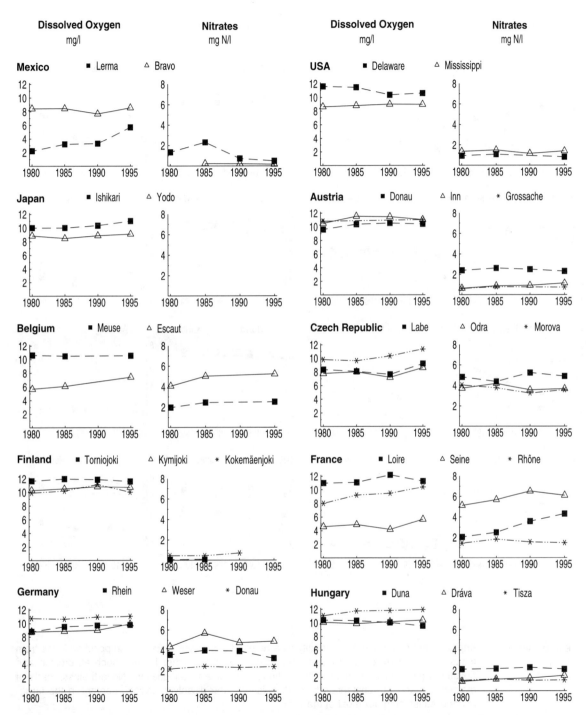

*Data refer to averages over three years of average annual concentrations. See Technical Annex for data sources, notes and comments.*

# 9 RIVER QUALITY

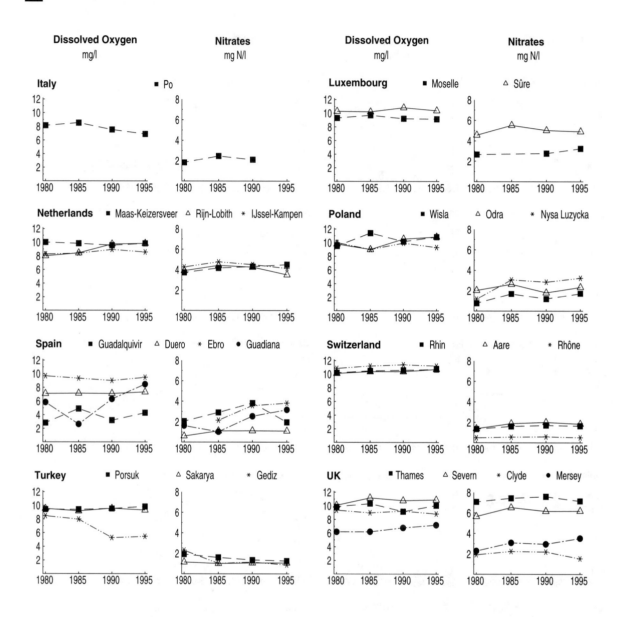

| Dissolved Oxygen mg/l | Nitrates mg N/l | Dissolved Oxygen mg/l | Nitrates mg N/l |

**Italy** ■ Po

**Netherlands** ■ Maas-Keizersveer  △ Rijn-Lobith  * IJssel-Kampen

**Spain** ■ Guadalquivir  △ Duero  * Ebro  ● Guadiana

**Turkey** ■ Porsuk  △ Sakarya  * Gediz

**Luxembourg** ■ Moselle  △ Sûre

**Poland** ■ Wisla  △ Odra  * Nysa Luzycka

**Switzerland** ■ Rhin  △ Aare  * Rhône

**UK** ■ Thames  △ Severn  * Clyde  ● Mersey

**STATE AND TRENDS SUMMARY**

Improvement in surface water quality as a result of significant reductions in pollution loads from industry and urban areas is not always easy to discern; other factors, such as erosion and pollution from diffuse sources, may continue to reduce water quality. Nevertheless, loads of oxygen demanding substances have diminished: the dissolved oxygen content in the larger rivers is satisfactory for most of the year.

While nitrate concentrations appear to have stabilised locally, probably as a result of nitrogen removal from sewage effluents or a reduction of fertiliser use, in many rivers the trend cannot yet be detected. Furthermore, success in cleaning up the worst polluted waters is sometimes achieved at the cost of failing to protect the few remaining pristine waters, so that all of a country's waters tend to be of average quality.

## WASTE WATER TREATMENT 10

### Sewerage and sewage treatment connection rates, mid-1990s*

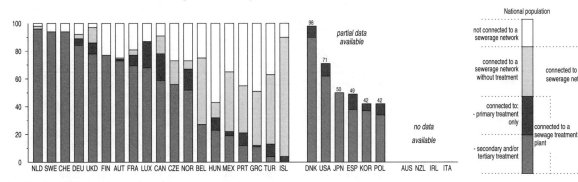

* or latest available year. Data prior to 1990 are not taken into account.

### Trends in sewage treatment connection rates
per cent of national population connected

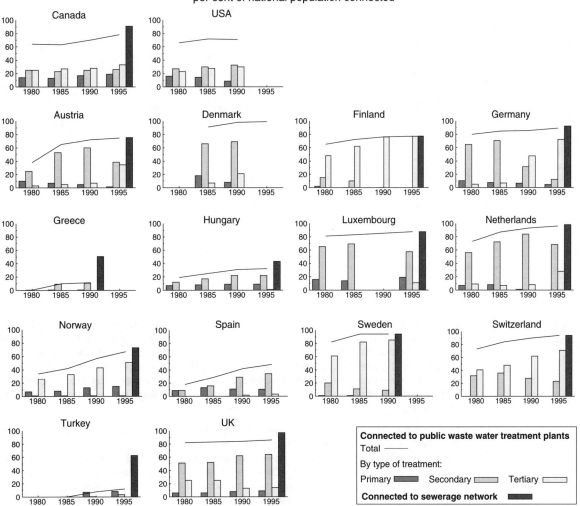

## 10 WASTE WATER TREATMENT

| | Waste water treatment Public sewage treatment connection rates | | | | | | | Sewerage network connection rates mid-1990s | Public expenditure on waste water treatment mid-1990s | |
|---|---|---|---|---|---|---|---|---|---|---|
| | early 1980s | | | mid-1990s | | | | | | |
| | Total | of which: | Secondary treatment | Tertiary treatment | Total | of which: | Secondary treatment | Tertiary treatment | Total | Total | of which: Investment |
| | % pop. | | % pop. | % pop. | % pop. | | % pop. | % pop. | % pop. | US$/capita | % |
| Canada ♦ | 64.0 | | 25.0 | 25.0 | 78.0 | | 26.0 | 33.0 | 91.0 | 66.9 | 60 |
| Mexico ♦ | .. | | .. | .. | 21.8 | | 19.2 | .. | 64.6 | 5.5 | 45 |
| USA ♦ | 65.8 | | 27.1 | 22.8 | .. | | .. | .. | .. | 105.0 | 47 |
| Japan ♦ | 30.0 | | 30.0 | .. | 50.1 | | 50.1 | .. | .. | .. | .. |
| Korea ♦ | .. | | .. | .. | 42.0 | | 37.0 | - | .. | 61.8 | 79 |
| Australia | .. | | .. | .. | .. | | .. | .. | .. | 41.7 | 68 |
| New Zealand | 59.0 | | 49.0 | - | .. | | .. | .. | .. | .. | .. |
| Austria | 38.0 | | 25.0 | 3.0 | 74.7 | | 38.6 | 34.7 | 75.5 | 133.8 | 68 |
| Belgium ♦ | 22.9 | | 22.9 | .. | 27.1 | | 27.1 | - | 75.4 | 51.7 | .. |
| Czech Rep. | 43.7 | | .. | .. | 56.0 | | .. | .. | 73.2 | .. | .. |
| Denmark ♦ | .. | | .. | .. | 99.0 | | .. | .. | .. | 56.7 | 51 |
| Finland ♦ | 65.0 | | 15.0 | 48.0 | 77.0 | | - | 77.0 | 77.3 | 49.7 | 47 |
| France ♦ | 61.5 | | .. | .. | 77.0 | | .. | .. | 81.0 | 105.8 | 36 |
| Germany ♦ | 79.9 | | 64.7 | 5.0 | 89.0 | | 12.2 | 72.2 | 92.2 | 111.2 | 62 |
| Greece | 0.5 | | 0.5 | .. | .. | | .. | .. | .. | 7.3 | .. |
| Hungary ♦ | 19.0 | | 12.0 | .. | 32.0 | | 22.0 | 1.0 | 43.0 | .. | .. |
| Iceland | .. | | - | - | 4.0 | | - | - | 90.0 | .. | .. |
| Ireland | 11.2 | | 11.0 | .. | .. | | .. | .. | 68.0 | .. | .. |
| Italy | 30.0 | | .. | .. | .. | | .. | .. | .. | 29.5 | 83 |
| Luxembourg | 81.0 | | 65.0 | .. | 87.5 | | 57.4 | 11.0 | 87.5 | .. | .. |
| Netherlands ♦ | 73.0 | | 56.0 | 9.0 | 96.0 | | 68.0 | 28.0 | 98.0 | 91.1 | 29 |
| Norway | 34.0 | | 1.0 | 26.0 | 67.0 | | 1.0 | 51.0 | 73.0 | 76.8 | 46 |
| Poland | .. | | .. | .. | 41.5 | | 29.7 | 4.1 | .. | .. | .. |
| Portugal ♦ | 2.3 | | .. | .. | .. | | .. | .. | .. | 32.4 | 80 |
| Spain | 17.9 | | 9.1 | .. | 48.3 | | 34.4 | 3.3 | .. | 24.4 | 65 |
| Sweden ♦ | 82.0 | | 20.0 | 61.0 | .. | | .. | .. | .. | 63.1 | 44 |
| Switzerland | 73.0 | | 32.0 | 41.0 | 94.0 | | 23.0 | 71.0 | 94.0 | 102.4 | 42 |
| Turkey ♦ | - | | - | .. | 12.1 | | 3.6 | .. | 62.5 | .. | .. |
| UK ♦ | 82.0 | | 51.0 | 25.0 | 86.0 | | 64.0 | 14.0 | 97.0 | 11.1 | 27 |
| **OECD ♦ | 50.8 | | .. | .. | 58.6 | | .. | .. | .. | .. | .. |

♦ *See Technical Annex for data sources, notes and comments.*

**STATE AND TRENDS SUMMARY**

OECD countries have progressed with basic domestic water pollution abatement: the share of the population connected to a waste water treatment plant rose from 50 per cent in the early 1980s to almost 60 per cent in the mid-1990s. The level of treatment varies significantly among OECD countries: secondary and tertiary treatment has progressed in some while primary treatment remains important in others. Some countries have reached the economic limit in terms of sewerage connection and must find other ways of serving small, isolated settlements.

The overall amount spent on sewerage and waste water treatment, and the relative shares of investment and operating expenditure within the total, also differ widely among countries. Some countries completed their sewer systems long ago and now face considerable investment to renew pipe networks. Other countries may recently have finished an expansion of waste water treatment capacity and the weight of expenditure has shifted to operating costs. Yet other countries must still complete their sewerage networks even as they build waste water treatment stations.

# WATER RESOURCES

*Freshwater resources are of major <u>environmental and economic importance</u>. Their distribution varies widely among and within countries. When consumers do not pay the full cost of water, they tend to use it inefficiently. This can result in serious problems, such as low river flows, water shortages, salinisation of freshwater bodies in coastal areas, human health problems, loss of wetlands, desertification and reduced food production. Pressures on water resources are exerted by overexploitation as well as by degradation of environmental quality. Relating resource abstraction to renewal of stocks is a central question concerning sustainable water resource management. If a significant share of a country's water comes from transboundary rivers, tensions between countries can arise, especially if water availability in the upstream country is less than in the downstream one.*

*<u>Sustainable management of water resources</u> has become a major concern in many countries: it can affect human health and the sustainability of agriculture. The efficiency of water use is key in matching supply and demand. Reducing losses, using more efficient technologies and recycling are all part of the solution, but applying the user pays principle to all types of users will be an essential element of sustainable management. <u>Performance</u> can be assessed against domestic objectives and international commitments. Agenda 21, adopted at UNCED (Rio de Janeiro, 1992), explicitly considers items such as the protection and preservation of freshwater resources. Water management is the focus of UNCSD's work in 1998.*

*<u>Indicators</u> presented here relate to:*

♦ *the <u>intensity of use</u> of water resources, expressed as gross abstractions in percentage of available freshwater resources and per capita;*

♦ *<u>prices for public water supply</u> to households, expressed in US dollars per cubic metre supplied. Abstractions for public water supply per capita are shown as complementary information.*

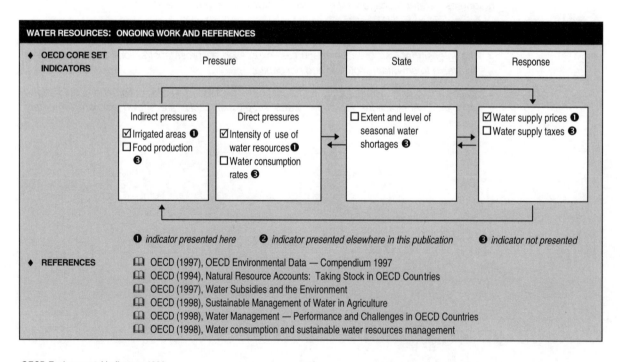

**WATER RESOURCES: ONGOING WORK AND REFERENCES**

♦ **OECD CORE SET INDICATORS**

| Pressure | State | Response |
|---|---|---|

**Indirect pressures**
☑ Irrigated areas ❶
☐ Food production ❸

**Direct pressures**
☑ Intensity of use of water resources ❶
☐ Water consumption rates ❸

☐ Extent and level of seasonal water shortages ❸

☑ Water supply prices ❶
☐ Water supply taxes ❸

❶ *indicator presented here*     ❷ *indicator presented elsewhere in this publication*     ❸ *indicator not presented*

♦ **REFERENCES**
   📖 OECD (1997), OECD Environmental Data — Compendium 1997
   📖 OECD (1994), Natural Resource Accounts: Taking Stock in OECD Countries
   📖 OECD (1997), Water Subsidies and the Environment
   📖 OECD (1998), Sustainable Management of Water in Agriculture
   📖 OECD (1998), Water Management — Performance and Challenges in OECD Countries
   📖 OECD (1998), Water consumption and sustainable water resources management

# INTENSITY OF USE OF WATER RESOURCES **11**

## Gross freshwater abstractions, mid-1990s

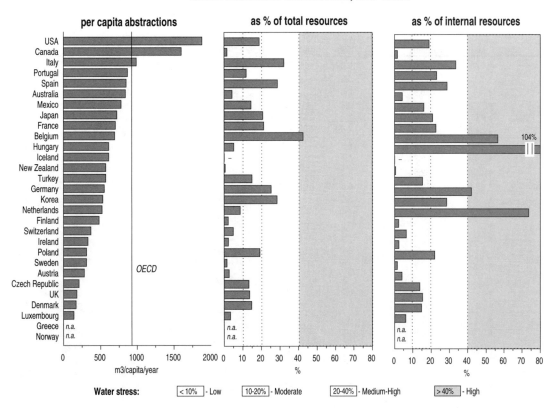

**per capita abstractions**    **as % of total resources**    **as % of internal resources**

Water stress:   | < 10% | - Low   | 10-20% | - Moderate   | 20-40% | - Medium-High   | > 40% | - High

## Freshwater abstractions by major uses

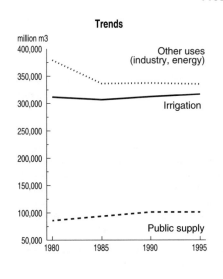

### Trends

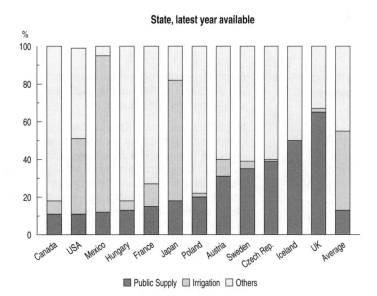

### State, latest year available

■ Public Supply   ▧ Irrigation   □ Others

## 11 INTENSITY OF USE OF WATER RESOURCES

| | | Intensity of use of water resources | | | Irrigation | | |
|---|---|---|---|---|---|---|---|
| | | abstractions as % of available resources | | abstractions per capita | | water abstractions per area of irrigated land | Irrigated areas as a share of cultivated land | |
| | | % mid-1990s | % change since 1980 | m3/cap/year mid-1990s | % change since 1980 | m3/ha/year 1995 | % 1995 | % change since 1980 |
| Canada | ♦ | 1.6 | 0.3 | 1600 | 5 | 4447 | 1.7 | 11 |
| Mexico | ♦ | 14.5 | 3.5 | 780 | -3 | 10033 | 24.7 | 21 |
| USA | ♦ | 18.9 | -2.0 | 1880 | -17 | 9019 | 11.4 | 6 |
| Japan | ♦ | 20.8 | 0.5 | 720 | -5 | 21519 | *61.1* | -2 |
| Korea | ♦ | 28.5 | 7.4 | 530 | 15 | 11161 | 65.0 | 9 |
| Australia | ♦ | 4.3 | 1.2 | 840 | 14 | 4548 | 4.9 | 48 |
| New Zealand | ♦ | 0.6 | 0.2 | 570 | 50 | 3860 | 69.5 | 72 |
| Austria | ♦ | 2.7 | 0.1 | 280 | -3 | .. | 0.3 | 8 |
| Belgium | ♦ | 42.5 | .. | 690 | .. | .. | *0.1* | *-14* |
| Czech Republic | ♦ | 15.3 | -5.8 | 240 | -27 | 531 | 3.7 | .. |
| Denmark | ♦ | 14.8 | -5.3 | 170 | -29 | 291 | 21.2 | 44 |
| Finland | ♦ | 2.2 | -1.1 | 480 | -38 | 313 | 2.5 | 8 |
| France | ♦ | 21.3 | 2.9 | 700 | 8 | 3020 | 8.4 | 81 |
| Germany | ♦ | 25.3 | *-0.1* | 550 | *-4* | 3320 | *4.0* | 9 |
| Greece | | .. | .. | .. | .. | .. | 37.9 | 55 |
| Hungary | ♦ | 5.2 | 1.2 | 610 | 36 | 1357 | 4.2 | 66 |
| Iceland | ♦ | 0.1 | - | 610 | 39 | - | - | - |
| Ireland | ♦ | 2.3 | 0.2 | 330 | 6 | .. | - | - |
| Italy | ♦ | 32.2 | - | 990 | -1 | .. | 24.3 | 26 |
| Luxembourg | ♦ | 3.4 | .. | 140 | .. | .. | .. | .. |
| Netherlands | ♦ | 8.6 | -1.5 | 520 | -20 | .. | 57.5 | 5 |
| Norway | | .. | .. | .. | .. | .. | 11.2 | 25 |
| Poland | ♦ | 19.2 | -3.4 | 310 | -23 | 2030 | 0.7 | 3 |
| Portugal | ♦ | 11.9 | .. | 870 | .. | 8095 | 21.8 | 9 |
| Spain | ♦ | 28.7 | -5.7 | 850 | -21 | 6838 | 17.5 | 19 |
| Sweden | ♦ | 1.5 | -0.8 | 310 | -37 | 924 | 3.8 | 64 |
| Switzerland | ♦ | 4.9 | - | 370 | -10 | .. | 5.4 | 6 |
| Turkey | ♦ | 15.0 | 8.1 | 570 | 58 | 5807 | 15.6 | 63 |
| UK | ♦ | *13.7* | *-6.1* | *180* | *-25* | *1352* | *2.1* | *-16* |
| OECD | ♦ | 11.3 | - | 930 | *-11* | .. | 11.5 | 15 |

♦ *See Technical Annex for data sources, notes and comments.*

**STATE AND TRENDS SUMMARY**

Irrigation, industry and household water use are generally pushing up demand for fresh water worldwide. It is estimated that global water demand has risen by more than double the rate of population growth in this century.

Most OECD countries increased their <u>water abstractions</u> over the 1970s and the early 1980s in response to demand by the agricultural and energy sectors. Since the late 1980s, some countries have stabilised their abstractions through more efficient irrigation techniques, the decline of water intensive industries (e.g. mining, steel), increased use of cleaner production technologies and reduced losses in pipe networks. Agriculture is the largest user of water worldwide. Global abstractions for irrigation have increased by over 60 per cent since 1960. In OECD countries overall, abstractions for irrigation mainly increased in the 1960s and the 1970s. In seven OECD countries, irrigation accounts for more than 50 per cent of total abstractions.

Although at national level most OECD countries show sustainable use of water resources, several countries have extensive arid or semi-arid regions where development is shaped by water scarcity. Indicators of <u>water resource use intensity</u> show great variations among and within individual countries. The national indicator may thus conceal unsustainable use in some regions and periods, and high dependence on water from other basins.

## PUBLIC WATER SUPPLY AND PRICE 🔢

**Abstractions for public supply per capita, mid 1990s**

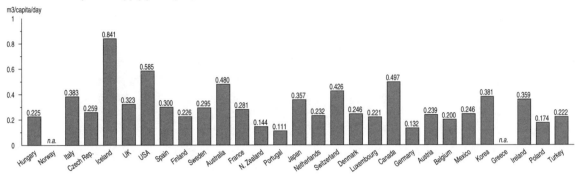

**Water prices in major selected cities, 1996**

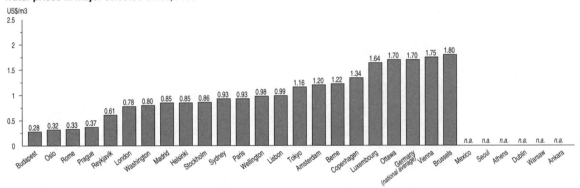

**Average prices for public freshwater supply to households, selected cities, 1996**

| | | Price US$/m3 | | | Price US$/m3 | | | Price US$/m3 | | | Price US$/m3 |
|---|---|---|---|---|---|---|---|---|---|---|---|
| Canada | Ottawa | 1.70 | Belgium | Brussels | 1.80 | Germany | (nat. average) ◆ | 1.70 | Portugal | Lisbon | 0.99 |
| | Toronto | 0.63 | | Antwerp | 0.97 | Hungary | Budapest | 0.28 | | Coimbra | 1.02 |
| | Winnipeg | 0.75 | | Liège | 1.50 | | Debrecen | 0.55 | | Porto | 0.98 |
| USA | Washington | 0.80 | Czech Rep. | Prague | 0.37 | | Pecs | 0.69 | Spain | Madrid | 0.85 |
| | New York | 0.88 | | Brno | 0.29 | Iceland | Reykjavik | 0.61 | | Barcelona | 0.81 |
| | Los Angeles | 0.60 | | Ostrava | 0.38 | | Hafnarfjorour | 0.51 | | Bilbao | 0.48 |
| Japan | Tokyo | 1.16 | Denmark | Copenhagen | 1.34 | Italy | Rome | 0.33 | Sweden | Stockholm | 0.86 |
| | Osaka | 0.70 | | Aarhus | 0.89 | | Bologna | 0.65 | | Goteborg | 0.58 |
| | Sapporo | 1.29 | | Odense | 0.98 | | Milan | 0.13 | | Malmo | 0.99 |
| Australia | Sydney | 0.93 | Finland | Helsinki | 0.85 | Luxembourg | Luxembourg | 1.64 | Switzerland | Berne | 1.22 |
| | Brisbane | 0.80 | | Tampere | 0.90 | Netherlands | Amsterdam | 1.20 | | Geneva | 2.25 |
| | Melbourne | 0.80 | | Vaasa | 1.32 | | The Hague | 1.92 | | Zurich | 2.26 |
| N. Zealand | Wellington ◆ | 0.98 | France | Paris | 0.93 | | Utrecht | 0.94 | UK | London ◆ | 0.78 |
| Austria | Vienna | 1.75 | | Bordeaux | 1.39 | Norway | Oslo ◆ | 0.32 | | Bristol ◆ | 0.78 |
| | Salzburg | 1.59 | | Lyon | 1.78 | | Bergen ◆ | 1.14 | | Manchester ◆ | 0.93 |
| | Linz | 1.11 | | | | | Trondheim ◆ | 1.05 | | | |

◆ *See Technical Annex for data sources, notes and comments.*

**STATE AND TRENDS**    Policies for pricing water supply and waste water treatment are important in matching supply and demand and improving the cost-effectiveness of water services. Prices charged to domestic and industrial users sometimes include an abstraction tax and increasingly cover full investment and operating costs. Domestic prices vary widely among and within countries. The cost of delivering clean water to urban areas depends, inter alia, on the proximity of water sources, the degree of purification needed and the settlement density of the area served.

# FOREST RESOURCES

*Forests are among the most diverse and widespread ecosystems on earth, and have many functions: they provide timber and other products; deliver recreation benefits and ecosystem services including regulation of soil, air and water; are reservoirs for biodiversity; and commonly act as carbon sinks. The impact from human activities on forest health and on natural forest growth and regeneration raises widespread concern. Many forest resources are threatened by overexploitation, degradation of environmental quality and conversion to other types of land uses. The main pressures result from human activities: they include agriculture expansion, transport infrastructure development, unsustainable forestry, air pollution and intentional burning of forests.*

*To be <u>sustainable</u>, forest management has to strive for maintaining timber value as well as environmental, social and aboriginal values. This includes optimal harvest rates, avoiding excessive use of the resource, and at the same time not setting harvest rates too low (particularly where age classes are unbalanced), which can reduce productive capacity. <u>Performance</u> can be assessed against national objectives and international principles on sustainable forest management adopted at UNCED (Rio de Janeiro, 1992). An international forest convention is under preparation. Other initiatives are the Helsinki process, which led to the European Criteria and Indicators for Sustainable Forest Management, and the Montreal process on Sustainable Development of Temperate and Boreal Forests.*

*<u>Indicators</u> presented here relate to:*

♦ *the <u>intensity of use of forest resources</u> (timber), relating annual productive capacity to actual harvest. Annual productive capacity is either a calculated value, such as annual allowable cut, or an estimate of annual growth for existing stock. The choice depends on forest characteristics and availability of information. NB: a measure based on a national average can conceal variations among forests. Changes in annual harvest, annual growth and growing stock are given as complementary information.*

♦ *<u>area of forest and wooded land</u>, as a percentage of total land area and per capita, along with changes in the area of forest and wooded land since 1970.*

*These indicators give insights into quantitative aspects of forest resources; they should be related to information on quality (e.g. species diversity, forest degradation) and on output of and trade in forest products.*

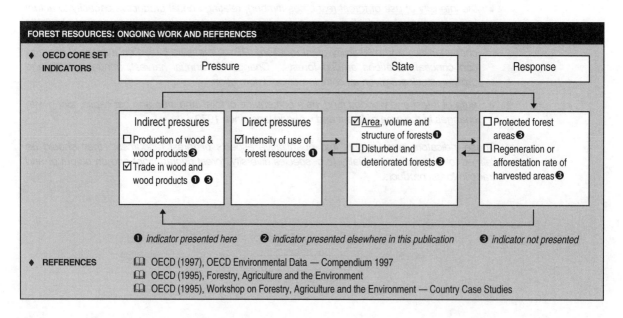

**FOREST RESOURCES: ONGOING WORK AND REFERENCES**

♦ **OECD CORE SET INDICATORS**

| Pressure | State | Response |
|---|---|---|

**Indirect pressures**
☐ Production of wood & wood products ❸
☑ Trade in wood and wood products ❶ ❸

**Direct pressures**
☑ Intensity of use of forest resources ❶

☑ <u>Area</u>, volume and structure of forests ❶
☐ Disturbed and deteriorated forests ❸

☐ Protected forest areas ❸
☐ Regeneration or afforestation rate of harvested areas ❸

❶ *indicator presented here*   ❷ *indicator presented elsewhere in this publication*   ❸ *indicator not presented*

♦ **REFERENCES**
📖 OECD (1997), OECD Environmental Data — Compendium 1997
📖 OECD (1995), Forestry, Agriculture and the Environment
📖 OECD (1995), Workshop on Forestry, Agriculture and the Environment — Country Case Studies

# INTENSITY OF USE OF FOREST RESOURCES 13

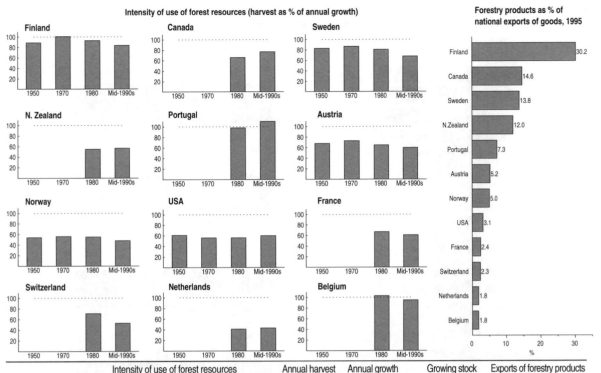

Intensity of use of forest resources (harvest as % of annual growth)

Forestry products as % of national exports of goods, 1995

| | Intensity of use of forest resources harvest as % of annual growth | | | | Annual harvest % change | Annual growth % change | Growing stock % change | Exports of forestry products % of national exports |
|---|---|---|---|---|---|---|---|---|
| | 1950s | 1970s | 1980s | mid-1990s | since 1980 | since 1980 | since 1980 | 1995 |
| Canada ♦ | .. | .. | 66 | 77 | 16.7 | 0.8 | 34.3 | 14.6 |
| Mexico ♦ | .. | .. | 23 | 17 | -35.1 | -10.4 | -6.5 | 0.4 |
| USA ♦ | 61 | 56 | 56 | 60 | 9.8 | 2.7 | 5.5 | 3.1 |
| Japan ♦ | .. | .. | 36 | 34 | -25.5 | -21.2 | 40.2 | 0.4 |
| Korea ♦ | .. | .. | .. | .. | -11.7 | .. | 40.6 | .. |
| Austria ♦ | 68 | 73 | 65 | 60 | 48.1 | 60.4 | 26.6 | 5.2 |
| Belgium ♦ | .. | .. | 103 | 95 | -4.4 | 3.6 | 31.5 | 1.8 |
| Czech Rep. | 81 | 68 | 80 | 69 | -9.3 | 5.2 | 11.0 | .. |
| Denmark ♦ | 85 | 118 | 75 | 58 | -13.4 | 12.2 | 69.4 | 1.2 |
| Finland ♦ | 89 | 101 | 93 | 84 | 7.9 | 20.1 | 19.1 | 30.2 |
| France ♦ | .. | .. | 67 | 61 | 30.0 | 42.3 | 21.0 | 2.4 |
| Germany ♦ | .. | .. | .. | .. | .. | .. | 41.8 | 1.6 |
| Greece ♦ | .. | .. | 71 | 54 | -20.6 | 2.9 | 14.3 | 0.8 |
| Hungary | .. | 60 | 70 | 53 | -19.8 | 5.8 | 21.9 | .. |
| Ireland | .. | 20 | 22 | .. | .. | .. | 37.2 | 0.5 |
| Italy ♦ | 107 | 53 | 64 | 28 | 8.4 | 146.3 | 118.6 | 1.4 |
| Luxembourg ♦ | .. | .. | 49 | 52 | 5.8 | -0.2 | 0.9 | 1.8 |
| Netherlands ♦ | .. | .. | 41 | 43 | 0.2 | -5.0 | 12.7 | 1.8 |
| Norway | 54 | 56 | 55 | 48 | 21.4 | 41.1 | 27.6 | 5.0 |
| Poland ♦ | .. | 53 | 65 | 56 | -0.4 | 14.8 | 34.3 | 0.4 |
| Portugal ♦ | .. | .. | 98 | 111 | 35.5 | 19.7 | 10.0 | 7.3 |
| Spain ♦ | .. | 59 | 46 | 52 | 94.3 | 72.7 | 40.1 | 1.7 |
| Sweden ♦ | 83 | 87 | 81 | 68 | -1.0 | 18.5 | 15.5 | 13.8 |
| Switzerland ♦ | .. | .. | 71 | 53 | -8.8 | 21.0 | 17.0 | 2.3 |
| Turkey ♦ | .. | 80 | 105 | 77 | -26.3 | - | - | 0.5 |
| UK ♦ | 100 | 63 | 41 | 45 | 45.9 | 30.4 | 21.8 | 0.7 |
| * **OECD ♦ | .. | .. | .. | 63 | 12.7 | .. | 20.2 | .. |

♦ *See Technical Annex for data sources, notes and comments.*

**STATE AND TRENDS SUMMARY**

Intensity of forest resource use does not show an increase for many OECD countries and has decreased in most countries from the 1950s. At national levels most OECD countries present a picture of sustainable use of their forest resources in quantitative terms, but with significant variations within countries.

## 14 FOREST AND WOODED LAND

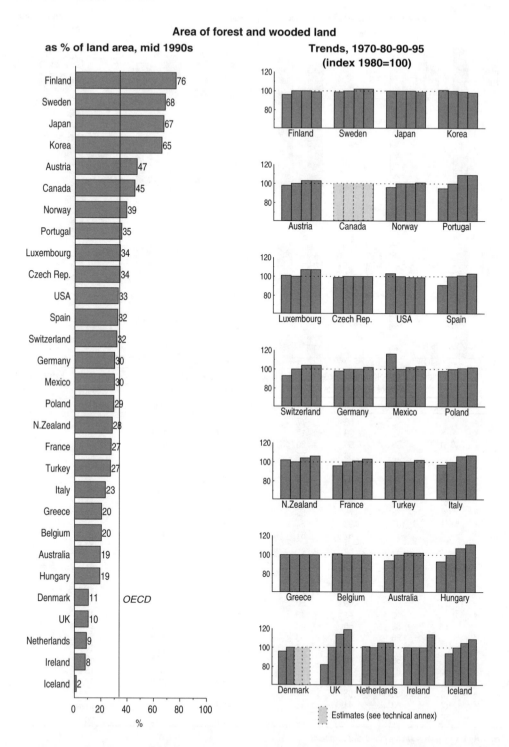

**Area of forest and wooded land**

**as % of land area, mid 1990s**

**Trends, 1970-80-90-95**
**(index 1980=100)**

**STATE AND TRENDS**
**SUMMARY**

The area of forests and wooded land has generally increased or remained stable at national level in most OECD countries and has remained stable in the OECD as a whole, but has decreased at world level.

# FISH RESOURCES

*Fish play key roles for human <u>food supply</u> and <u>aquatic ecosystems</u>.  Coastal development and environmental quality constitute significant pressures on fish stocks. Overexploitation affects both freshwater and marine fish stocks. Aquaculture has been developed to an extent where its dependence on fishmeal products puts it in competition with other commercial markets and could become a limiting factor of aquaculture development.*

*The <u>sustainable management</u> of fish resources has become a major concern.  With continual growth in fish catches, some 80 per cent of the more valuable stocks are overfished and new or less valuable species are being exploited as several fish stocks have collapsed. Thus a central issue for sustainable management of catchment areas is whether resource abstraction exceeds the renewal of the stocks over an extended period. <u>Performance</u> can be assessed against domestic objectives and bilateral and multilateral agreements such as those on conservation and use of fish resources (Atlantic Ocean, Pacific Ocean, Baltic Sea, etc.), the Rome Consensus on world fisheries, the Code of Conduct for Responsible Fishing (FAO, November 1995), the UN Convention on the Law of the Sea and its implementation agreement on straddling and highly migratory fish stocks.*

*<u>Indicators</u> presented here relate to:*

♦ *<u>national fish catches</u> expressed as per cent of world captures and as amounts per capita, and related changes since 1980.  National fish consumption (food supply from fish per capita) is given as additional information.*

♦ *<u>global and regional fish catches</u> and related changes since 1980. Changes in the proportion of fish resources under various phases of fishery development are given as additional information.*

*These indicators give insights into quantitative aspects of fish resources;  they should be related to information on the status of fish stocks.*

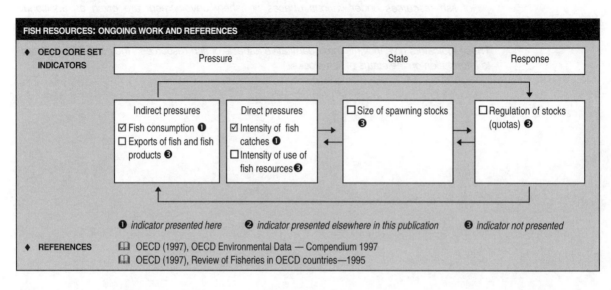

**FISH RESOURCES: ONGOING WORK AND REFERENCES**

| OECD CORE SET INDICATORS | Pressure | | State | Response |
|---|---|---|---|---|

| | Indirect pressures | Direct pressures | ☐ Size of spawning stocks ❸ | ☐ Regulation of stocks (quotas) ❸ |
|---|---|---|---|---|
| | ☑ Fish consumption ❶ <br> ☐ Exports of fish and fish products ❸ | ☑ Intensity of fish catches ❶ <br> ☐ Intensity of use of fish resources ❸ | | |

❶ *indicator presented here*       ❷ *indicator presented elsewhere in this publication*       ❸ *indicator not presented*

**◆ REFERENCES**       📖 OECD (1997), OECD Environmental Data — Compendium 1997
📖 OECD (1997), Review of Fisheries in OECD countries—1995

## FISH CATCHES AND CONSUMPTION: NATIONAL 15

### Fish catches in marine and inland waters

### Fish consumption per capita

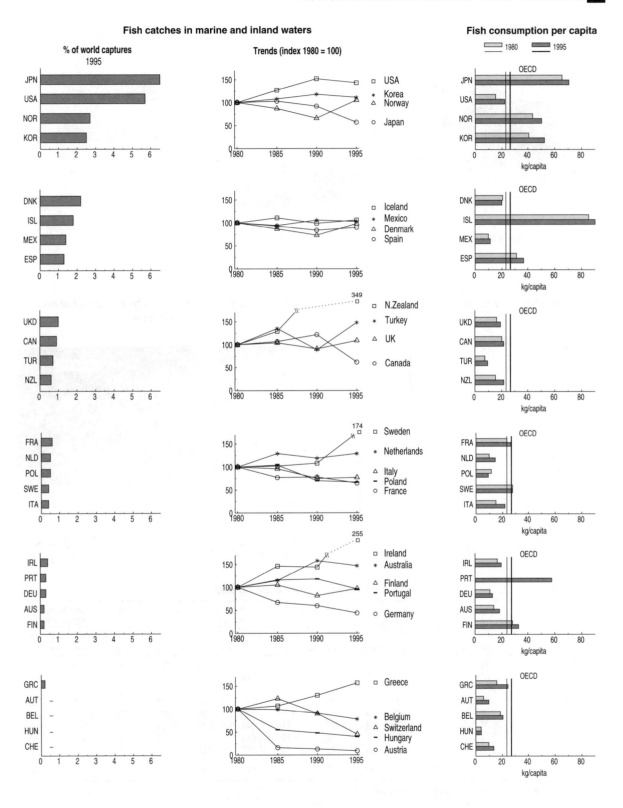

**% of world captures**
1995

**Trends (index 1980 = 100)**

□ 1980   ■ 1995

## 16 FISH CATCHES AND CONSUMPTION: GLOBAL AND REGIONAL

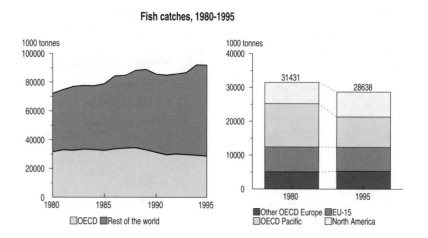

**Fish catches, 1980-1995**

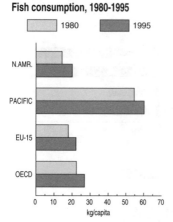

**Fish consumption, 1980-1995**

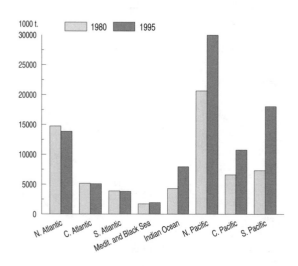

**Fish catches by major marine fishing area**

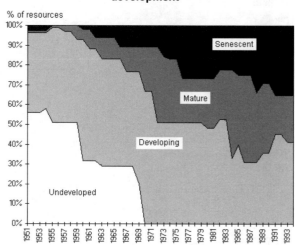

**World marine fish resources by phase of fishery development**

### Fish catches by major marine fishing area

| | Total | | share of world catches | | Cod, hake, haddock | | Herring, sardine, anchovy | | Jack, mullet, saury | | Tuna, bonito, billfish, etc. | |
|---|---|---|---|---|---|---|---|---|---|---|---|---|
| | 1 000 t. | % change | % | % | 1 000 t. | % change | 1 000 t. | % change | 1 000 t. | % change | 1 000 t. | % change |
| | 1995 | since 1980 | 1980 | 1995 | 1995 | since 1980 | 1995 | since 1980 | 1995 | since 1980 | 1995 | since 1980 |
| Northern Atlantic | 13 841 | - 6 | 23 | 15 | 3 265 | - 37 | 3 475 | 68 | 1 363 | - 51 | 62 | 8 |
| Central Atlantic | 5 089 | - 2 | 8 | 6 | 33 | - 37 | 2 178 | 7 | 380 | - 48 | 390 | 11 |
| Southern Atlantic | 3 819 | - 2 | 6 | 4 | 1 116 | 43 | 587 | - 41 | 376 | - 50 | 123 | 70 |
| Mediterr. & Black Sea | 1 921 | 13 | 3 | 2 | 92 | 76 | 817 | - 10 | 123 | - 7 | 61 | 35 |
| Indian Ocean | 7 945 | 85 | 7 | 9 | 4 | 118 | 706 | 25 | 689 | 109 | 1 100 | 273 |
| Northern Pacific | 29 973 | 45 | 32 | 33 | 5 327 | 24 | 2 043 | - 37 | 1 895 | 108 | 670 | 37 |
| Central Pacific | 10 740 | 63 | 10 | 12 | 0 | - 79 | 1 650 | 10 | 1 198 | 95 | 2 174 | 83 |
| Southern Pacific | 18 031 | 146 | 11 | 20 | 781 | 176 | 10 557 | 155 | 5 096 | 282 | 202 | 32 |
| Total | 91 359 | 42 | 100 | 100 | 10 617 | - 1 | 22 014 | 43 | 11 120 | 47 | 4 783 | 80 |

♦ *See Technical Annex for data sources, notes and comments.*

## FISH CATCHES AND CONSUMPTION 15&16

| | Total fish catches | | | | | Marine fish catches | Fish consumption | |
| | Total | | per capita | | share of world catches | share of total catches | per capita | |
| | 1 000 t. | % change | kg/cap. | % change | % | % | kg/cap. | % change |
| | 1995 | since 1980 | 1995 | since 1980 | 1995 | 1995 | 1995 | since 1980 |
|---|---|---|---|---|---|---|---|---|
| Canada | 835 | - 38 | 28.2 | -49 | 0.9 | 89 | 21.4 | 7 |
| Mexico | 1 290 | 3 | 13.6 | -24 | 1.4 | 91 | 11.2 | 15 |
| USA | 5 221 | 43 | 19.8 | 24 | 5.7 | 89 | 22.0 | 45 |
| Japan | 5 937 | - 43 | 47.3 | -47 | 6.5 | 92 | 70.6 | 8 |
| Korea | 2 320 | 11 | 51.4 | -6 | 2.5 | 99 | 52.3 | 29 |
| Australia | 194 | 47 | 10.8 | 20 | 0.2 | 99 | 18.2 | 31 |
| New Zealand | 544 | 249 | 152.0 | 207 | 0.6 | 99 | 21.5 | 41 |
| Austria | - | - 91 | - | -91 | - | n.app. | 9.7 | 69 |
| Belgium ◆ | 36 | - 22 | 3.4 | -24 | - | 99 | 20.4 | 11 |
| Czech Rep. | 1 | .. | 0.1 | - | - | n.app. | 4.9 | 26 |
| Denmark ◆ | 1 999 | - 2 | 382.4 | -4 | 2.2 | 100 | 19.9 | -3 |
| Finland | 167 | - 3 | 32.8 | -9 | 0.2 | 61 | 33.0 | 17 |
| France | 513 | - 35 | 8.8 | -40 | 0.6 | 99 | 26.4 | 13 |
| Germany | 240 | - 56 | 2.9 | -58 | 0.3 | 90 | 12.9 | 17 |
| Greece | 166 | 57 | 15.8 | 45 | 0.2 | 89 | 24.3 | 56 |
| Hungary | 13 | - 60 | 1.3 | -58 | - | n.app. | 4.0 | 1 |
| Iceland | 1 607 | 6 | 6039.5 | -9 | 1.8 | 100 | 92.1 | 8 |
| Ireland | 381 | 155 | 105.8 | 141 | 0.4 | 99 | 19.5 | 19 |
| Italy | 390 | - 23 | 6.8 | -24 | 0.4 | 97 | 21.7 | 47 |
| Netherlands | 438 | 29 | 28.3 | 18 | 0.5 | 99 | 14.4 | 48 |
| Norway | 2 525 | 5 | 580.7 | -1 | 2.7 | 100 | 50.2 | 15 |
| Poland | 426 | - 33 | 11.0 | -39 | 0.5 | 93 | 9.1 | -20 |
| Portugal | 261 | - 4 | 26.3 | -5 | 0.3 | 100 | 57.7 | .. |
| Spain | 1 182 | - 10 | 30.1 | -14 | 1.3 | 100 | 36.9 | 18 |
| Sweden | 405 | 74 | 45.7 | 63 | 0.4 | 99 | 27.7 | 0 |
| Switzerland | 2 | - 55 | 0.2 | -59 | - | n.app. | 13.4 | 38 |
| Turkey | 631 | 48 | 10.2 | 6 | 0.7 | 95 | 9.4 | 30 |
| UK | 910 | 9 | 15.5 | 5 | 1.0 | 100 | 19.0 | 18 |
| OECD | 28 638 | - 9 | 26.4 | -19 | 31.1 | 95 | 26.9 | 20 |
| World | 91 972 | 28 | 16.2 | - | 100.0 | 91 | 13.4 | 18 |

◆ *See Technical Annex for data sources, notes and comments.*    *.. not available   - nil or negligible   n.app. not applicable*

**STATE AND TRENDS SUMMARY**

Of 200 stocks fished worldwide, more than 25 per cent are estimated to be overexploited, depleted or recovering, while about 38 per cent are fully exploited.

Trend analysis shows large differences among OECD countries and among fishing areas, with high increases in some areas (e.g. the Pacific and Indian Oceans) and decreases in others (e.g. the North Atlantic).

The intensity of national catches per unit of GDP and per capita varies widely among OECD countries, reflecting the share of fisheries and associated industries in the economy.

# BIODIVERSITY

*Biodiversity can be defined as the variety of and variability among living organisms, both diversity at the ecosystem and species levels and genetic diversity within species. Conservation of biodiversity has become a key concern nationally and globally. Pressures on biodiversity can be physical (e.g. habitat alteration and fragmentation through changes in land use and land cover conversions), chemical (e.g. pollution from human activities) or biological (e.g. alteration of population dynamics and species structure through the release of exotic species or the commercial use of wildlife resources).*

*The conservation and sustainable use of biodiversity form an integral part of sustainable development, encompassing the integration of biodiversity concerns into economic policies as well as measures to protect areas, habitats and species. Protection levels range from full to partial protection in actual protected areas to promotion of biodiversity conservation outside such areas (e.g. on farms or in forests). Performance can be assessed against domestic objectives and international agreements such as: the Convention on Biological Diversity (Rio de Janeiro, 1992), the Convention on the Conservation of Migratory Species of Wild Animals (Bonn, 1979), the Convention on International Trade in Endangered Species of Wild Fauna and Flora (CITES, Washington, 1973), the Convention on Wetlands of International Importance (Ramsar, 1971) and the Convention on the Conservation of European Wildlife and Natural Habitats (Bern, 1979).*

*Indicators presented here relate to the conservation of biodiversity and concern:*

- ♦ *the number of threatened or extinct species compared to the number of known species. "Threatened" refers to the "endangered" and "vulnerable" categories, i.e. species in danger of extinction and species soon likely to be in danger of extinction. Data cover mammals, birds, fish, reptiles, amphibians and vascular plants. Other major groups (e.g. invertebrates, fungi) are not covered at the present time.*

- ♦ *protected areas, i.e. land areas under management categories I to VI of the World Conservation Union (IUCN) classification, which refer to different levels of protection. Categories I and II (wilderness areas, strict nature reserves and national parks) reflect the highest protection level. Protected areas are a form of defence against change in land use and in other human activities, which, if unsustainable, can pose a threat to ecosystems and landscapes, and lead to biodiversity changes including natural habitat loss.*

*These indicators need to be complemented with indicators on the sustainable use of biodiversity as a resource.*

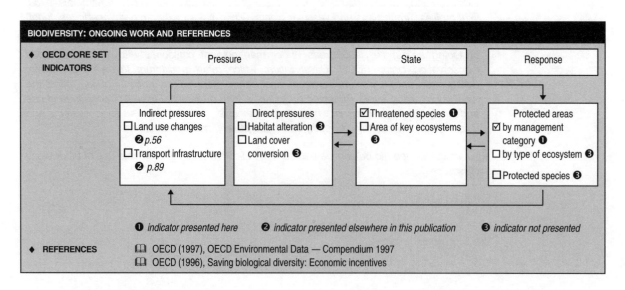

**BIODIVERSITY: ONGOING WORK AND REFERENCES**

◆ **OECD CORE SET INDICATORS**

| Pressure | State | Response |
|---|---|---|

| Indirect pressures | Direct pressures | ☑ Threatened species ❶ | Protected areas |
|---|---|---|---|
| ☐ Land use changes ❷ *p.56* | ☐ Habitat alteration ❸ | ☐ Area of key ecosystems ❸ | ☑ by management category ❶ |
| ☐ Transport infrastructure ❷ *p.89* | ☐ Land cover conversion ❸ | | ☐ by type of ecosystem ❸ |
| | | | ☐ Protected species ❸ |

❶ *indicator presented here*  ❷ *indicator presented elsewhere in this publication*  ❸ *indicator not presented*

◆ **REFERENCES**  📖 OECD (1997), OECD Environmental Data — Compendium 1997
📖 OECD (1996), Saving biological diversity: Economic incentives

## THREATENED SPECIES **17**

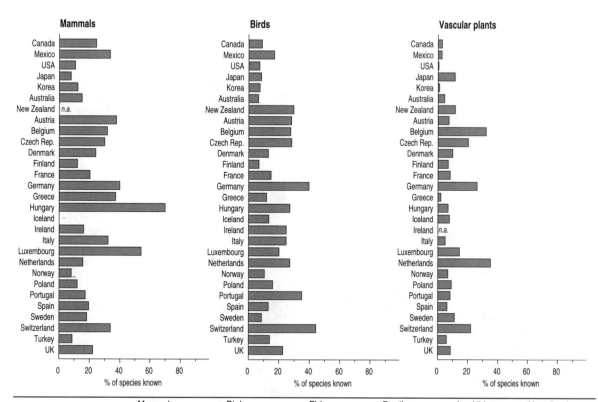

**Mammals** — % of species known

**Birds** — % of species known

**Vascular plants** — % of species known

| | | Mammals | | Birds | | Fish | | Reptiles | | Amphibians | | Vascular plants | |
|---|---|---|---|---|---|---|---|---|---|---|---|---|---|
| | | species known | species threatened | species known | species threatened | species known | species threatened | species known | species threatened | species known | species threatened | species known | species threatened |
| | | number | % | number | % | number | % | number | % | number | % | number | % |
| Canada | ♦ | 193 | 24 | 514 | 9 | 276 | 22 | 43 | 28 | 42 | 10 | 3300 | 3 |
| Mexico | ♦ | 486 | 34 | 1052 | 17 | 2110 | 6 | 703 | 18 | 289 | 17 | 18000 | 2 |
| USA | ♦ | 466 | 11 | 1090 | 7 | 2640 | 2 | 368 | 7 | 222 | 4 | 22200 | 1 |
| Japan | ♦ | 183 | 8 | 652 | 8 | 198 | 11 | 87 | 3 | 59 | 10 | 7266 | 11 |
| Korea | ♦ | 99 | 12 | 312 | 7 | 134 | 7 | 26 | 38 | 15 | 40 | 3969 | 1 |
| Australia | | 315 | 15 | 777 | 6 | 4195 | 0.4 | 770 | 7 | 203 | 14 | 25000 | 4 |
| New Zealand | ♦ | 5 | .. | 149 | 30 | 27 | 37 | 45 | 49 | 3 | 100 | 2200 | 9-14 |
| Austria | ♦ | 88 | 38 | 228 | 28 | 73 | 42 | 14 | 100 | 19 | 95 | 2900 | 7 |
| Belgium | ♦ | 57 | 32 | 167 | 28 | 46 | 54 | 4 | 50 | 13 | 31 | 1202 | 32 |
| Czech Rep. | ♦ | 87 | 30 | 220 | 28 | 65 | 6 | 13 | 62 | 20 | 65 | 2500 | 20 |
| Denmark | ♦ | 50 | 24 | 170 | 13 | 33 | 18 | 5 | - | 14 | 29 | 1200 | 10 |
| Finland | ♦ | 59 | 12 | 234 | 7 | 60 | 12 | 5 | 20 | 5 | 20 | 1305 | 7 |
| France | ♦ | 119 | 20 | 354 | 15 | 426 | 6 | 36 | 17 | 36 | 31 | 4762 | 8 |
| Germany | ♦ | 93 | 40 | 273 | 40 | 66 | 68 | 12 | 75 | 19 | 58 | 2954 | 26 |
| Greece | ♦ | 116 | 37 | 407 | 12 | 111 | 37 | 58 | 5 | 16 | - | 6000 | 2 |
| Hungary | ♦ | 83 | 70 | 214 | 27 | 82 | 20 | 16 | 100 | 16 | 100 | 2510 | 7 |
| Iceland | ♦ | 4 | - | 75 | 13 | 5 | - | - | .. | - | .. | 485 | 8 |
| Ireland | | 31 | 16 | 146 | 25 | .. | .. | 1 | - | 3 | 33 | .. | .. |
| Italy | ♦ | 118 | 32 | 473 | 25 | 85 | .. | 58 | 22 | 38 | 24 | 5599 | 5 |
| Luxembourg | | 61 | 54 | 270 | 20 | 34 | 38 | 6 | 100 | 13 | 100 | 1054 | 15 |
| Netherlands | ♦ | 64 | 16 | 170 | 27 | 28 | 82 | 7 | 86 | 16 | 56 | 1392 | 35 |
| Norway | ♦ | 50 | 8 | 222 | 10 | 191 | - | 5 | 20 | 5 | 40 | 1310 | 7 |
| Poland | ♦ | 84 | 12 | 232 | 16 | 48 | 25 | 9 | 33 | 18 | 100 | 2300 | 9 |
| Portugal | ♦ | 99 | 17 | 312 | 35 | 43 | 19 | 34 | 9 | 18 | - | 3095 | 8 |
| Spain | ♦ | 118 | 19 | 368 | 13 | 68 | 26 | 56 | 18 | 25 | 8 | 8000 | 6 |
| Sweden | ♦ | 66 | 18 | 245 | 9 | 150 | 5 | 7 | - | 13 | 54 | 1900 | 11 |
| Switzerland | ♦ | 80 | 34 | 197 | 44 | 47 | 45 | 14 | 79 | 17 | 94 | 2617 | 22 |
| Turkey | ♦ | 128 | 9 | 295 | 14 | 441 | 2 | 106 | 5 | 21 | 5 | 8575 | 6 |
| UK | ♦ | 63 | 22 | 517 | 23 | 54 | 11 | 7 | 43 | 7 | 29 | 2297 | 8 |

♦ *See Technical Annex for data sources, notes and comments.*

# 18 PROTECTED AREAS

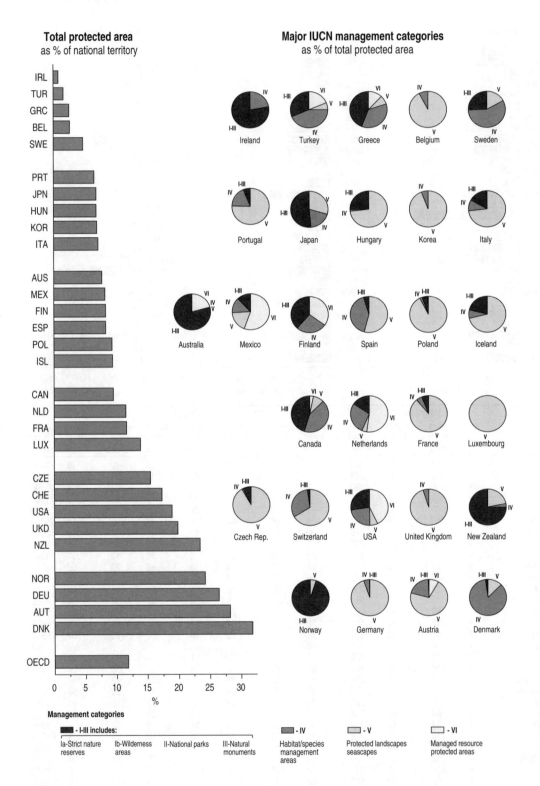

**Total protected area**
as % of national territory

**Major IUCN management categories**
as % of total protected area

Management categories

- I-III includes:

Ia-Strict nature reserves  Ib-Wilderness areas  II-National parks  III-Natural monuments

- IV Habitat/species management areas

- V Protected landscapes seascapes

- VI Managed resource protected areas

## PROTECTED AREAS 18

| | | Major protected areas, 1996 | | | | Strict nature reserves, wilderness areas, national parks, 1996 | | | |
|---|---|---|---|---|---|---|---|---|---|
| | | Number of sites | Total size 1 000 km² | % of territory | per capita km²/1 000 inh. | Number of sites | Total size 1 000 km² | % of territory | per capita km²/1 000 inh. |
| Canada | | 807 | 945 | 9 | 32 | 375 | 427 | 4 | 14 |
| Mexico | ♦ | 114 | 160 | 8 | 2 | 42 | 20 | 1.0 | 0.2 |
| USA | ♦ | 1701 | 1772 | 19 | 7 | 572 | 431 | 5 | 2 |
| Japan | | 65 | 26 | 7 | 0.2 | 23 | 13 | 3 | 0.1 |
| Korea | | 26 | 7 | 7 | 0.1 | - | - | - | - |
| Australia | ♦ | 5606 | 598 | 8 | 33 | 2650 | 470 | 6 | 26 |
| New Zealand | | 224 | 63 | 23 | 17 | 65 | 44 | 16 | 12 |
| Austria | | 177 | 24 | 28 | 3 | 2 | 0.2 | 0.2 | - |
| Belgium | | 4 | 0.8 | 3 | 0.1 | - | - | - | - |
| Czech Rep. | | 44 | 12 | 16 | 1.2 | 6 | 0.9 | 1.1 | 0.1 |
| Denmark | ♦ | 116 | 14 | 32 | 3 | 9 | 0.2 | 0.6 | - |
| Finland | | 137 | 28 | 8 | 5 | 43 | 11 | 3 | 2 |
| France | ♦ | 132 | 64 | 12 | 1.1 | 8 | 4 | 0.7 | 0.1 |
| Germany | | 525 | 94 | 26 | 1.2 | 3 | 0.4 | 0.1 | - |
| Greece | | 34 | 3 | 3 | 0.3 | 9 | 1.3 | 1.0 | 0.1 |
| Hungary | | 54 | 6 | 7 | 0.6 | 5 | 2 | 2 | 0.2 |
| Iceland | | 26 | 10 | 9 | 36 | 4 | 2 | 2 | 7 |
| Ireland | | 15 | 0.6 | 0.8 | 0.2 | 5 | 0.5 | 0.7 | 0.1 |
| Italy | | 170 | 21 | 7 | 0.4 | 10 | 4 | 1.2 | 0.1 |
| Luxembourg | | 1 | 0.4 | 14 | 0.9 | - | - | - | - |
| Netherlands | ♦ | 78 | 5 | 12 | 0.3 | 15 | 0.5 | 1.2 | - |
| Norway | ♦ | 128 | 94 | 24 | 21 | 89 | 89 | 23 | 20 |
| Poland | | 106 | 29 | 9 | 0.8 | 16 | 2 | 0.5 | - |
| Portugal | ♦ | 26 | 6 | 6 | 0.6 | 4 | 0.3 | 0.4 | - |
| Spain | ♦ | 219 | 42 | 8 | 1.1 | 13 | 2 | 0.4 | 0.1 |
| Sweden | | 182 | 21 | 5 | 2 | 19 | 5 | 1.2 | 0.6 |
| Switzerland | | 107 | 7 | 17 | 1.0 | 1 | 0.2 | 0.4 | - |
| Turkey | | 63 | 13 | 2 | 0.2 | 23 | 4 | 0.5 | 0.1 |
| UK | | 153 | 49 | 20 | 0.8 | - | - | - | - |
| OECD | | 11040 | 4114 | 12 | 4 | 4011 | 1534 | 4 | 1.4 |
| World | | 16428 | 12633 | 9 | 2 | 5776 | 5583 | 4 | 1.0 |

♦ *See Technical Annex for data sources, notes and comments.*

**STATE AND TRENDS SUMMARY**

Protected areas have grown significantly since 1980 in almost all countries, reaching 12 per cent of total area for the OECD as a whole.

Actual protection levels and related trends are difficult to evaluate, as protected areas change over time: new areas are designated, boundaries are revised and some sites may be destroyed or changed by pressures from economic development or natural processes. Environmental performance depends both on the designation of the area (e.g. the representativeness of species or ecosystems protected) and on management effectiveness.

# III. SOCIO-ECONOMIC INDICATORS

# GDP AND POPULATION

*Economic activity is a key determinant of <u>sustainable development</u> and its economic, social and environmental dimensions. Economic growth and production patterns have major effects on environmental issues and on environmental <u>performance</u>. They imply use of energy and other natural resource assets, as well as pollutant discharges and waste production. The sustainability of development depends on the evolution of the stock and quality of natural resources or "natural capital" and on pollution constraints. Economic growth also provides opportunities to finance public expenditure for environmental protection and to replace man-made capital, thus introducing cleaner, less resource-intensive technologies and environmentally friendly goods.*

*Population influences production and consumption patterns, and hence the <u>sustainability</u> of development. It is an important determinant of environmental conditions and trends. Population density implies density of human activity. Overall population growth puts pressure on natural resources and adds to the challenge of providing sanitation and other environmental infrastructure. Population also affects the environment in the ways that its structural elements (age classes, active population, size of households, etc.) influence consumption patterns and waste production.*

<u>*Indicators*</u> *presented here relate to:*

- *<u>gross domestic product</u> (GDP), in total and per capita, as well as the change in GDP compared to the change in population over the same period.*

- *<u>population growth and density</u>, presenting changes in national resident population, as well as population densities and an "ageing index" (the ratios between the population over 64 and under 15).*

**GDP AND POPULATION: REFERENCES**

📖 OECD (1997), OECD Environmental Data — Compendium 1997

📖 OECD (1997), OECD Economic Outlook

📖 OECD (1998), National Accounts of OECD Countries, Vol.1, 1960/1996: Main Aggregates

📖 OECD (1997), Quarterly Labour Force Statistics

📖 OECD (1998), Main Economic Indicators

## GROSS DOMESTIC PRODUCT 19

### GDP per capita, change since 1980 (%)

| | |
|---|---|
| Poland | .. |
| Mexico | -2.2 |
| Turkey | 47.6 |
| Hungary | .. |
| Czech Rep. | .. |
| Greece | 17.5 |
| Portugal | 45.9 |
| Korea | 206.0 |
| Spain | 39.6 |
| New Zealand | 24.6 |
| Ireland | 85.2 |
| Finland | 27.1 |
| UK | 34.9 |
| Sweden | 17.5 |
| w.Germany | 28.4 |
| Italy | 30.4 |
| Netherlands | 29.3 |
| Belgium | 25.6 |
| Austria | 28.6 |
| Australia | 31.4 |
| Iceland | 21.0 |
| France | 24.8 |
| Denmark | 34.5 |
| Canada | 19.5 |
| Japan | 52.6 |
| Switzerland | 10.0 |
| Norway | 49.0 |
| USA | 28.4 |
| Luxembourg | 81.8 |

### GDP per capita, state, 1996

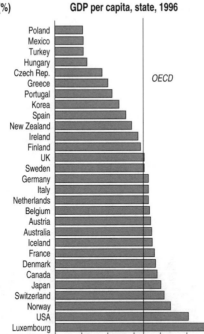

### % change GDP - % change population

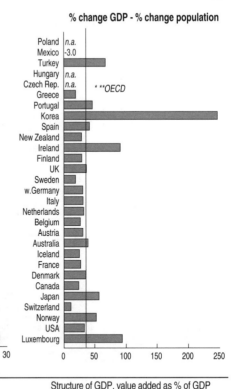

| | Gross Domestic Product | | | Structure of GDP, value added as % of GDP | | |
|---|---|---|---|---|---|---|
| | Total Billion US$ 1996 | per capita 1 000 US$/cap. 1996 | % change GDP- % change population 1996-1980 | Agriculture % mid-1990s | Industry % mid-1990s | Services % mid-1990s |
| Canada | 581.7 | 19.4 | 23.7 | 2.1 | 25.7 | 72.2 |
| Mexico | 523.6 | 5.4 | -3.0 | 5.0 | 25.5 | 69.5 |
| USA | 6722.5 | 25.3 | 33.1 | 1.8 | 27.9 | 70.3 |
| Japan | 2533.5 | 20.1 | 56.7 | 1.9 | 38.0 | 60.1 |
| Korea | 556.0 | 12.2 | 246.1 | 6.5 | 43.3 | 50.2 |
| Australia | 335.9 | 18.4 | 39.1 | 3.4 | 27.1 | 69.5 |
| New Zealand | 53.2 | 14.6 | 28.5 | 8.3 | 25.1 | 66.6 |
| Austria | 147.2 | 18.2 | 30.7 | 1.5 | 30.5 | 68.0 |
| Belgium | 183.2 | 18.0 | 26.4 | 1.3 | 28.0 | 70.7 |
| Czech Rep. | 93.3 | 9.0 | .. | 4.1 | 37.5 | 58.4 |
| Denmark | 100.3 | 19.1 | 35.5 | 3.6 | 24.3 | 72.1 |
| Finland | 83.5 | 16.3 | 29.0 | 3.7 | 31.4 | 64.9 |
| France | 1103.2 | 18.9 | 26.9 | 2.4 | 26.5 | 71.1 |
| Germany ♦ | 1459.6 | 17.8 | *30.6* | *1.0* | *36.1* | *62.9* |
| Greece | 105.9 | 10.1 | 19.0 | 12.0 | 20.0 | 68.0 |
| Hungary ♦ | 62.1 | 6.1 | .. | 7.2 | 31.8 | 61.0 |
| Iceland | 5.0 | 18.5 | 24.9 | 8.9 | 21.9 | 69.2 |
| Ireland | 57.2 | 15.8 | 90.7 | 5.7 | 36.2 | 58.1 |
| Italy | 1024.4 | 17.8 | 30.9 | 2.9 | 31.6 | 65.5 |
| Luxembourg | 11.9 | 28.5 | 93.7 | 1.0 | 24.0 | 75.0 |
| Netherlands | 276.3 | 17.8 | 32.1 | 3.1 | 27.1 | 69.8 |
| Norway | 95.5 | 21.9 | 52.4 | 2.5 | 29.9 | 67.6 |
| Poland ♦ | 205.4 | 5.3 | .. | 7.6 | 39.3 | 53.1 |
| Portugal | 108.2 | 10.9 | 46.4 | 3.7 | 33.4 | 62.9 |
| Spain | 529.2 | 13.5 | 41.6 | 2.9 | 31.7 | 65.4 |
| Sweden | 151.3 | 17.0 | 18.7 | 2.0 | 27.5 | 70.5 |
| Switzerland | 147.0 | 20.7 | 11.1 | 3.0 | 33.5 | 63.5 |
| Turkey | 341.3 | 5.4 | 67.2 | 15.7 | 31.8 | 52.5 |
| UK | 997.5 | 17.0 | 36.5 | 1.7 | 27.1 | 71.2 |
| OECD ♦ | 18595.0 | 17.0 | *35.5* | *2.6* | *30.2* | *67.1* |

♦ See Technical Annex for data sources, notes and comments.

# 20 POPULATION GROWTH AND DENSITY

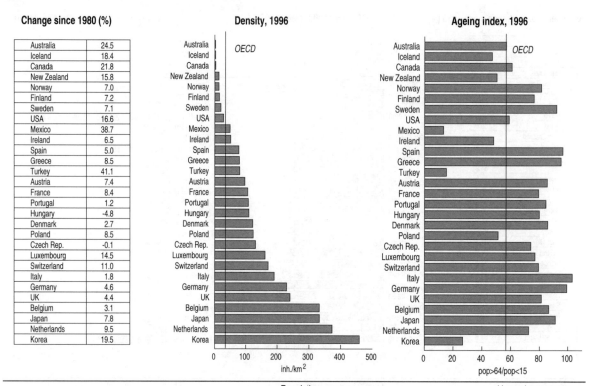

| Change since 1980 (%) | |
|---|---|
| Australia | 24.5 |
| Iceland | 18.4 |
| Canada | 21.8 |
| New Zealand | 15.8 |
| Norway | 7.0 |
| Finland | 7.2 |
| Sweden | 7.1 |
| USA | 16.6 |
| Mexico | 38.7 |
| Ireland | 6.5 |
| Spain | 5.0 |
| Greece | 8.5 |
| Turkey | 41.1 |
| Austria | 7.4 |
| France | 8.4 |
| Portugal | 1.2 |
| Hungary | -4.8 |
| Denmark | 2.7 |
| Poland | 8.5 |
| Czech Rep. | -0.1 |
| Luxembourg | 14.5 |
| Switzerland | 11.0 |
| Italy | 1.8 |
| Germany | 4.6 |
| UK | 4.4 |
| Belgium | 3.1 |
| Japan | 7.8 |
| Netherlands | 9.5 |
| Korea | 19.5 |

Density, 1996 — inh./km²

Ageing index, 1996 — pop>64/pop<15

| | Population | | | | Unemployment rate |
|---|---|---|---|---|---|
| | Total 1 000 inh. | Density inh./km² | Ageing index pop>64/pop<15 | | % of total labour force |
| | 1996 | 1996 | 1996 | 1980 | 1996 |
| Canada | 29955 | 3.0 | 60.7 | 41.3 | 9.7 |
| Mexico | 96582 | 49.3 | 13.2 | 8.8 | 5.5 |
| USA | 265557 | 28.4 | 58.7 | 50.1 | 5.4 |
| Japan | 125864 | 333.1 | 91.2 | 38.4 | 3.3 |
| Korea | 45545 | 458.8 | 26.7 | 12.1 | 2.0 |
| Australia | 18289 | 2.4 | 56.8 | 38.1 | 8.5 |
| New Zealand | 3640 | 13.5 | 50.2 | 35.7 | 6.1 |
| Austria | 8106 | 96.7 | 85.4 | 75.5 | 6.2 |
| Belgium | 10157 | 332.7 | 86.6 | 71.8 | 12.9 |
| Czech Rep. | 10316 | 130.8 | 73.9 | 57.7 | 3.5 |
| Denmark | 5262 | 122.1 | 85.7 | 69.0 | 8.8 |
| Finland | 5125 | 15.2 | 76.1 | 58.8 | 16.3 |
| France | 58380 | 105.9 | 79.3 | 62.2 | 12.4 |
| Germany | 81877 | 229.4 | 99.3 | 85.4 | 10.3 |
| Greece | 10465 | 79.3 | 95.2 | 57.6 | 10.4 |
| Hungary | 10193 | 109.6 | 79.8 | .. | 10.6 |
| Iceland | 270 | 2.6 | 47.0 | 35.9 | 4.3 |
| Ireland | 3621 | 51.5 | 48.0 | 35.3 | 11.3 |
| Italy | 57459 | 190.7 | 103.1 | 62.8 | 12.1 |
| Luxembourg | 418 | 161.6 | 76.8 | 73.5 | 3.3 |
| Netherlands | 15494 | 373.1 | 72.4 | 51.6 | 6.7 |
| Norway | 4370 | 13.5 | 81.3 | 66.6 | 4.9 |
| Poland | 38618 | 123.5 | 51.1 | 41.6 | 12.4 |
| Portugal | 9935 | 108.0 | 84.5 | 44.9 | 7.3 |
| Spain | 39270 | 77.6 | 96.5 | 41.9 | 22.7 |
| Sweden | 8901 | 19.8 | 92.1 | 83.1 | 8.0 |
| Switzerland | 7085 | 171.6 | 79.3 | 70.2 | 4.7 |
| Turkey | 62695 | 80.4 | 15.2 | 12.1 | 6.5 |
| UK | 58782 | 240.0 | 81.3 | 71.2 | 7.4 |
| OECD | 1092231 | 31.4 | 56.8 | 42.9 | 7.5 |

◆ See Technical Annex for data sources, notes and comments.

# CONSUMPTION

*Consumption by households and government is a determinant of sustainable development and its economic, environmental and social dimensions. It has important implications for the level and pattern of production and for related demands for natural resources. Growth of private consumption has both positive and negative environmental effects, entailing increased use of private transport, more leisure and tourism, higher energy consumption, increased use of packaged goods and higher waste production, but also demand for environmentally friendly goods.*

*Agenda 21, adopted at UNCED (Rio de Janeiro, 1992), stresses that changes in consumption and production patterns are necessary to ensure more <u>sustainable development</u>. These can be promoted by increasing consumer awareness and expanding use of approaches such as life cycle analysis of products and extended producer responsibility. Governments can show the way by "greening" their own consumption and operations.*

<u>*Indicators*</u> *presented here relate to:*

♦ <u>*private consumption*</u>*, i.e. by households and private non-profit institutions serving households. They present private final consumption expenditure expressed as percentage of GDP and per capita, as well as the structure of private consumption.*

♦ <u>*government consumption*</u>*, presenting government final consumption expenditure expressed as percentage of GDP and per capita.*

*They should be read in conjunction with other indicators in this publication, notably those dealing with energy, transport, waste and water, and should be complemented with information on production patterns and trends.*

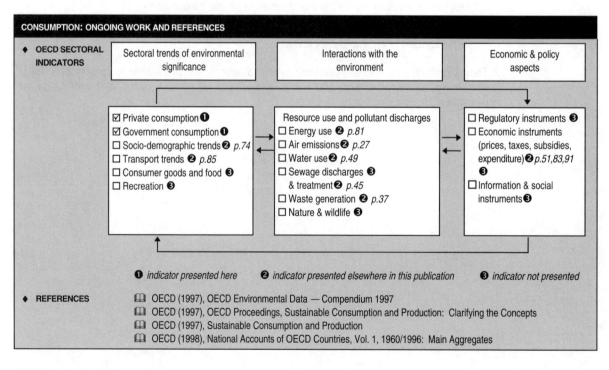

**CONSUMPTION: ONGOING WORK AND REFERENCES**

♦ **OECD SECTORAL INDICATORS**

| Sectoral trends of environmental significance | Interactions with the environment | Economic & policy aspects |
|---|---|---|

| | | |
|---|---|---|
| ☑ Private consumption ❶<br>☑ Government consumption ❶<br>☐ Socio-demographic trends ❷ *p.74*<br>☐ Transport trends ❷ *p.85*<br>☐ Consumer goods and food ❸<br>☐ Recreation ❸ | Resource use and pollutant discharges<br>☐ Energy use ❷ *p.81*<br>☐ Air emissions ❷ *p.27*<br>☐ Water use ❷ *p.49*<br>☐ Sewage discharges ❸<br>  & treatment ❷ *p.45*<br>☐ Waste generation ❷ *p.37*<br>☐ Nature & wildlife ❸ | ☐ Regulatory instruments ❸<br>☐ Economic instruments<br>  (prices, taxes, subsidies,<br>  expenditure) ❷ *p.51,83,91*<br>  ❸<br>☐ Information & social<br>  instruments ❸ |

❶ *indicator presented here*     ❷ *indicator presented elsewhere in this publication*    ❸ *indicator not presented*

♦ **REFERENCES**
📖 OECD (1997), OECD Environmental Data — Compendium 1997
📖 OECD (1997), OECD Proceedings, Sustainable Consumption and Production: Clarifying the Concepts
📖 OECD (1997), Sustainable Consumption and Production
📖 OECD (1998), National Accounts of OECD Countries, Vol. 1, 1960/1996: Main Aggregates

## PRIVATE CONSUMPTION 21

### Private final consumption expenditure, 1996

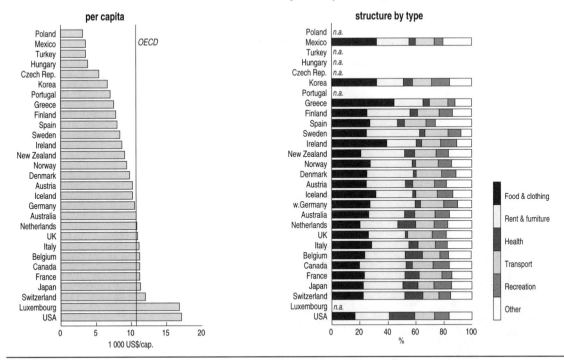

per capita — 1 000 US$/cap.

structure by type — %

Food & clothing / Rent & furniture / Health / Transport / Recreation / Other

| | Total | per capita | | Consumption patterns, by type, % | | | | | |
|---|---|---|---|---|---|---|---|---|---|
| | % of GDP 1996 | 1 000 US$/cap. 1996 | % change since 1980 | Food & clothing | Rent & furniture | Health | Transport | Recreation | Other |
| | | | Private final consumption expenditure | | | | | | |
| Canada | 57 | 11.2 | 19.7 | 19.8 | 33.1 | 4.5 | 14.7 | 11.8 | 16.0 |
| Mexico | 65 | 3.5 | -7.1 | 32.1 | 23.2 | 4.6 | 13.3 | 6.3 | 20.5 |
| USA | 68 | 17.1 | 33.7 | 16.6 | 24.1 | 18.4 | 14.0 | 10.6 | 16.4 |
| Japan | 56 | 11.3 | 51.3 | 22.5 | 28.1 | 10.8 | 11.3 | 12.9 | 14.4 |
| Korea | 54 | 6.6 | 180.4 | 32.1 | 19.1 | 6.6 | 13.5 | 13.0 | 15.7 |
| Australia | 58 | 10.7 | 32.1 | 26.4 | 25.5 | 7.3 | 14.4 | 10.5 | 15.8 |
| New Zealand | 62 | 9.1 | 20.9 | 20.9 | 31.1 | 7.2 | 15.2 | 9.0 | 16.7 |
| Austria | 56 | 10.2 | 33.1 | 24.8 | 27.7 | 5.3 | 15.5 | 8.5 | 18.3 |
| Belgium | 62 | 11.2 | 23.1 | 23.6 | 28.7 | 12.3 | 12.4 | 6.3 | 16.2 |
| Czech Rep. | 60 | 5.4 | .. | .. | .. | .. | .. | .. | .. |
| Denmark | 52 | 9.8 | 29.8 | 25.2 | 33.0 | 2.1 | 18.0 | 10.6 | 11.1 |
| Finland | 48 | 7.8 | 25.3 | 25.3 | 30.6 | 5.4 | 15.3 | 9.8 | 13.5 |
| France | 59 | 11.2 | 28.8 | 23.3 | 28.8 | 10.2 | 16.1 | 7.4 | 14.2 |
| Germany ♦ | 59 | 10.5 | *28.8* | *27.3* | *32.2* | *3.8* | *16.6* | *10.1* | *9.9* |
| Greece | 74 | 7.5 | 31.1 | 44.4 | 20.8 | 4.5 | 13.3 | 5.3 | 11.6 |
| Hungary | 63 | 3.8 | .. | .. | .. | .. | .. | .. | .. |
| Iceland | 55 | 10.2 | 19.0 | 31.5 | 26.3 | 2.2 | 15.2 | 11.4 | 13.4 |
| Ireland | 55 | 8.7 | 47.7 | 39.1 | 21.2 | 3.9 | 13.4 | 11.9 | 10.4 |
| Italy | 62 | 11.1 | 34.1 | 28.4 | 26.6 | 6.5 | 12.2 | 8.7 | 17.6 |
| Luxembourg | 59 | 16.8 | 38.5 | .. | .. | .. | .. | .. | .. |
| Netherlands | 61 | 10.8 | 21.8 | 20.2 | 26.7 | 12.9 | 13.1 | 9.9 | 17.2 |
| Norway | 43 | 9.4 | 33.0 | 27.6 | 29.8 | 2.5 | 16.0 | 9.8 | 14.3 |
| Poland | 59 | 3.1 | .. | .. | .. | .. | .. | .. | .. |
| Portugal | 64 | 7.0 | 46.9 | .. | .. | .. | .. | .. | .. |
| Spain | 59 | 8.0 | 31.1 | 27.3 | 19.5 | 5.1 | 15.4 | 6.6 | 26.1 |
| Sweden | 49 | 8.4 | 8.4 | 24.9 | 37.8 | 3.9 | 16.5 | 9.4 | 7.5 |
| Switzerland | 58 | 12.0 | 8.2 | 22.4 | 29.6 | 12.9 | 11.3 | 8.6 | 15.2 |
| Turkey | 65 | 3.5 | 20.7 | .. | .. | .. | .. | .. | .. |
| UK | 64 | 10.9 | 45.3 | 26.2 | 26.2 | 1.7 | 17.4 | 10.2 | 18.3 |
| OECD ♦ | 62 | 10.6 | *32.5* | .. | .. | .. | .. | .. | .. |

♦ *See Technical Annex for data sources, notes and comments.*

## 22 GOVERNMENT CONSUMPTION

**Government final consumption expenditure**

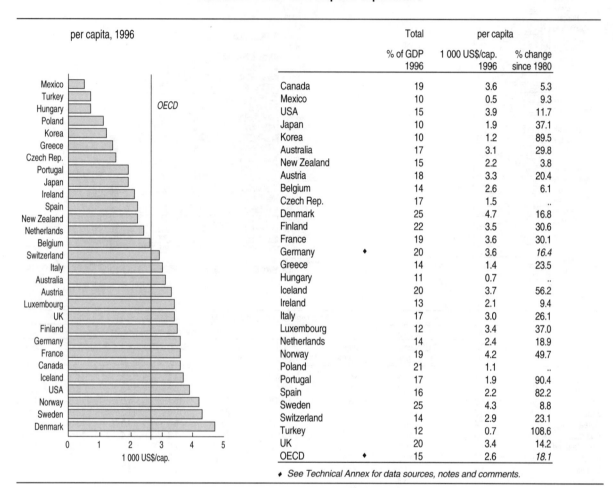

per capita, 1996

| | Total | per capita | |
|---|---|---|---|
| | % of GDP 1996 | 1 000 US$/cap. 1996 | % change since 1980 |
| Canada | 19 | 3.6 | 5.3 |
| Mexico | 10 | 0.5 | 9.3 |
| USA | 15 | 3.9 | 11.7 |
| Japan | 10 | 1.9 | 37.1 |
| Korea | 10 | 1.2 | 89.5 |
| Australia | 17 | 3.1 | 29.8 |
| New Zealand | 15 | 2.2 | 3.8 |
| Austria | 18 | 3.3 | 20.4 |
| Belgium | 14 | 2.6 | 6.1 |
| Czech Rep. | 17 | 1.5 | .. |
| Denmark | 25 | 4.7 | 16.8 |
| Finland | 22 | 3.5 | 30.6 |
| France | 19 | 3.6 | 30.1 |
| Germany ♦ | 20 | 3.6 | *16.4* |
| Greece | 14 | 1.4 | 23.5 |
| Hungary | 11 | 0.7 | .. |
| Iceland | 20 | 3.7 | 56.2 |
| Ireland | 13 | 2.1 | 9.4 |
| Italy | 17 | 3.0 | 26.1 |
| Luxembourg | 12 | 3.4 | 37.0 |
| Netherlands | 14 | 2.4 | 18.9 |
| Norway | 19 | 4.2 | 49.7 |
| Poland | 21 | 1.1 | .. |
| Portugal | 17 | 1.9 | 90.4 |
| Spain | 16 | 2.2 | 82.2 |
| Sweden | 25 | 4.3 | 8.8 |
| Switzerland | 14 | 2.9 | 23.1 |
| Turkey | 12 | 0.7 | 108.6 |
| UK | 20 | 3.4 | 14.2 |
| OECD ♦ | 15 | 2.6 | *18.1* |

♦ *See Technical Annex for data sources, notes and comments.*

# ENERGY

*Energy is a major component of OECD economies, both as a sector in itself and as a factor input to all other economic activities.  Energy production and use have environmental effects that differ greatly by energy source.  Fuel combustion is the main source of local and regional air pollution and greenhouse gas emissions;  other effects involve water quality, land use, risks related to the nuclear fuel cycle and risks related to the extraction, transport and use of fossil fuels.*

*The structure of a country's energy supply and the intensity of its energy use, along with changes over time, are key determinants of environmental performance and sustainability of economic development.  The supply structure varies considerably among countries.  It is influenced by demand from industry, transport and households, by national energy policies and by national and international energy prices.*

*Indicators presented here relate to:*

♦ *trends in energy intensities.  Energy intensities, expressed as energy supply per unit of GDP and per capita, reflect, at least partly, changes in energy efficiency and thus are a key policy option to reduce atmospheric emissions.*

♦ *energy mix, i.e. the structure of and changes in energy supply, in terms of primary energy source as a percentage of total energy supply.  This is closely related to consumption and production patterns and to environmental effects.*

♦ *energy prices for industry and households, with changes in real energy end-use prices.*

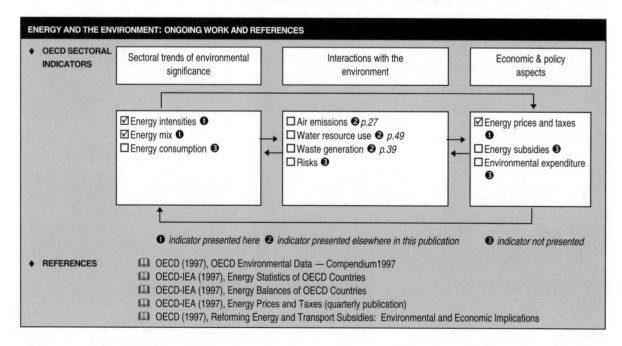

**ENERGY AND THE ENVIRONMENT: ONGOING WORK AND REFERENCES**

♦ **OECD SECTORAL INDICATORS**

| Sectoral trends of environmental significance | Interactions with the environment | Economic & policy aspects |
|---|---|---|
| ☑ Energy intensities ❶<br>☑ Energy mix ❶<br>☐ Energy consumption ❸ | ☐ Air emissions ❷ *p.27*<br>☐ Water resource use ❷ *p.49*<br>☐ Waste generation ❷ *p.39*<br>☐ Risks ❸ | ☑ Energy prices and taxes ❶<br>☐ Energy subsidies ❸<br>☐ Environmental expenditure ❸ |

❶ *indicator presented here* ❷ *indicator presented elsewhere in this publication*     ❸ *indicator not presented*

♦ **REFERENCES**

📖 OECD (1997), OECD Environmental Data — Compendium1997
📖 OECD-IEA (1997), Energy Statistics of OECD Countries
📖 OECD-IEA (1997), Energy Balances of OECD Countries
📖 OECD-IEA (1997), Energy Prices and Taxes (quarterly publication)
📖 OECD (1997), Reforming Energy and Transport Subsidies: Environmental and Economic Implications

## State, 1995

### Energy supply per unit of GDP    Energy supply per capita

### Trends, 1980-1995
■ per unit of GDP   □ per capita

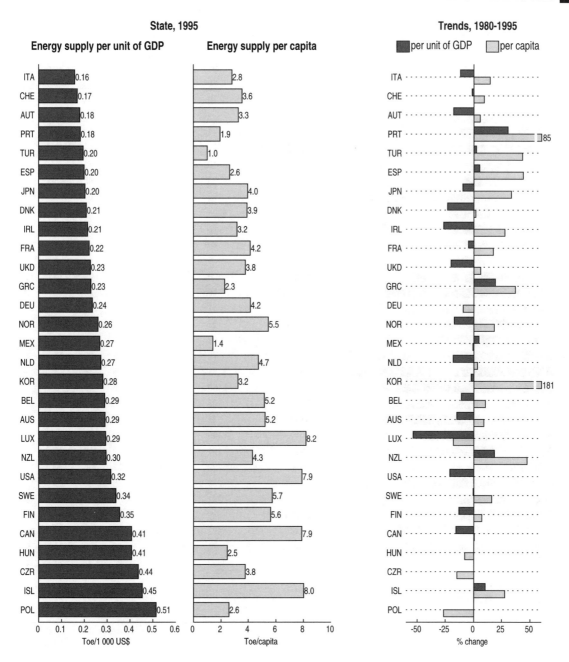

**STATE AND TRENDS SUMMARY**

During the 1980s, energy intensity per unit of GDP generally decreased for OECD countries overall as a consequence of economic structural changes and energy conservation measures. Progress in per capita terms has been much slower, reflecting an overall increase in energy supply.

Variations among OECD countries are wide (from 1 to 3 per unit of GDP, from 1 to 8 per capita) and depend both on national economic structure and geography (e.g. climate).

# 24 ENERGY MIX

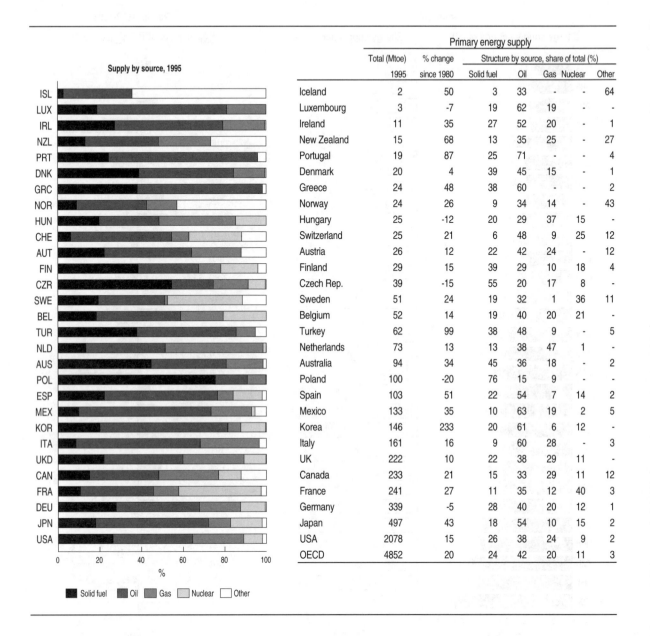

Supply by source, 1995

| | Primary energy supply | | | | | | |
|---|---|---|---|---|---|---|---|
| | Total (Mtoe) | % change | Structure by source, share of total (%) | | | | |
| | 1995 | since 1980 | Solid fuel | Oil | Gas | Nuclear | Other |
| Iceland | 2 | 50 | 3 | 33 | - | - | 64 |
| Luxembourg | 3 | -7 | 19 | 62 | 19 | - | - |
| Ireland | 11 | 35 | 27 | 52 | 20 | - | 1 |
| New Zealand | 15 | 68 | 13 | 35 | 25 | - | 27 |
| Portugal | 19 | 87 | 25 | 71 | - | - | 4 |
| Denmark | 20 | 4 | 39 | 45 | 15 | - | 1 |
| Greece | 24 | 48 | 38 | 60 | - | - | 2 |
| Norway | 24 | 26 | 9 | 34 | 14 | - | 43 |
| Hungary | 25 | -12 | 20 | 29 | 37 | 15 | - |
| Switzerland | 25 | 21 | 6 | 48 | 9 | 25 | 12 |
| Austria | 26 | 12 | 22 | 42 | 24 | - | 12 |
| Finland | 29 | 15 | 39 | 29 | 10 | 18 | 4 |
| Czech Rep. | 39 | -15 | 55 | 20 | 17 | 8 | - |
| Sweden | 51 | 24 | 19 | 32 | 1 | 36 | 11 |
| Belgium | 52 | 14 | 19 | 40 | 20 | 21 | - |
| Turkey | 62 | 99 | 38 | 48 | 9 | - | 5 |
| Netherlands | 73 | 13 | 13 | 38 | 47 | 1 | - |
| Australia | 94 | 34 | 45 | 36 | 18 | - | 2 |
| Poland | 100 | -20 | 76 | 15 | 9 | - | - |
| Spain | 103 | 51 | 22 | 54 | 7 | 14 | 2 |
| Mexico | 133 | 35 | 10 | 63 | 19 | 2 | 5 |
| Korea | 146 | 233 | 20 | 61 | 6 | 12 | - |
| Italy | 161 | 16 | 9 | 60 | 28 | - | 3 |
| UK | 222 | 10 | 22 | 38 | 29 | 11 | - |
| Canada | 233 | 21 | 15 | 33 | 29 | 11 | 12 |
| France | 241 | 27 | 11 | 35 | 12 | 40 | 3 |
| Germany | 339 | -5 | 28 | 40 | 20 | 12 | 1 |
| Japan | 497 | 43 | 18 | 54 | 10 | 15 | 2 |
| USA | 2078 | 15 | 26 | 38 | 24 | 9 | 2 |
| OECD | 4852 | 20 | 24 | 42 | 20 | 11 | 3 |

■ Solid fuel  ■ Oil  ■ Gas  ▨ Nuclear  ☐ Other

**STATE AND TRENDS SUMMARY**

The energy supply mix has a major effect on environmental performance because the environmental impact of each energy source differs greatly.

During the 1980s and early 1990s, growth in total primary energy supply was accompanied by changes in the fuel mix: the shares of solid fuels and oil fell, while those of gas and other sources rose. This trend is particularly visible in OECD Europe. The rates of change, however, vary widely by country.

## Trends in real energy end-use prices (Index 1980 = 100)

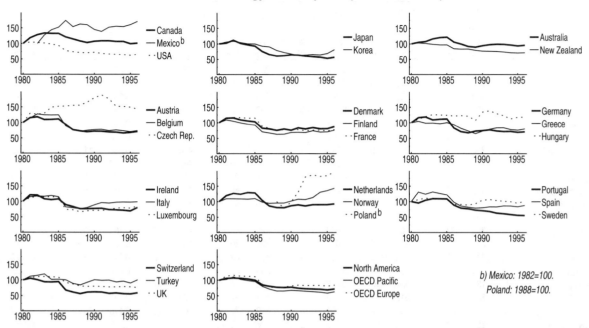

b) Mexico: 1982=100.
Poland: 1988=100.

## Selected energy prices for industry and households, mid-1990s

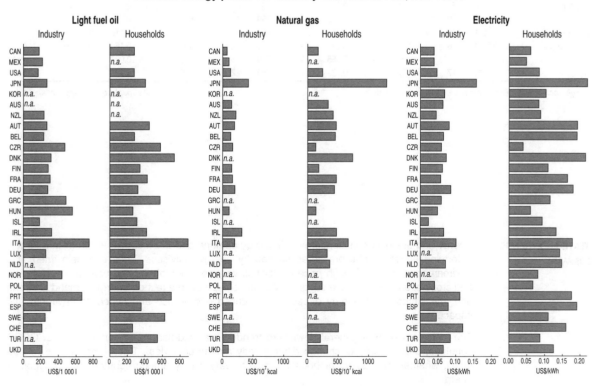

## 25 ENERGY PRICES

| | | Industry | | | | | Households | | | | | | Real energy |
|---|---|---|---|---|---|---|---|---|---|---|---|---|---|
| | | Oil | | Natural gas | | Electricity | | Oil | | Natural gas | | Electricity | | end-use prices |
| | | Price US$/1 000l. 1996 | Tax (%) 1996 | Price US$/10⁷kcal 1996 | Tax (%) 1996 | Price US$/kWh 1996 | Tax (%) 1996 | Price US$/1 000l. 1996 | Tax (%) 1996 | Price US$/10⁷kcal 1996 | Tax (%) 1996 | Price US$/kWh 1996 | Tax (%) 1996 | Change (%) since 1980 |
| Canada | | 179 | .. | 71 | .. | 0.038 | .. | 281 | .. | 170 | .. | 0.060 | .. | 1.4 |
| Mexico | ♦ | 217 | 12 | 103 | 13 | 0.038 | 13 | .. | .. | .. | .. | 0.048 | 13 | 70.6 |
| USA | | 169 | .. | 128 | .. | 0.046 | .. | 279 | .. | 242 | .. | 0.084 | .. | -35.1 |
| Japan | | 269 | 3 | 423 | 3 | 0.157 | 6 | 407 | 3 | 1294 | 3 | 0.230 | 5 | -43.4 |
| Korea | | .. | .. | .. | .. | 0.068 | .. | .. | .. | .. | .. | 0.103 | .. | -18.6 |
| Australia | | .. | .. | 146 | .. | 0.063 | .. | .. | .. | 333 | .. | 0.083 | .. | -4.5 |
| New Zealand | | 236 | - | 217 | 6 | 0.044 | - | .. | .. | 416 | 14 | 0.088 | 11 | -28.2 |
| Austria | | 269 | 19 | 195 | - | 0.081 | - | 452 | 39 | 468 | 17 | 0.192 | 17 | -29.2 |
| Belgium | | 233 | 8 | 133 | - | 0.065 | - | 282 | 24 | 452 | 21 | 0.191 | 18 | -26.6 |
| Czech Republic | | 475 | 59 | 164 | - | 0.059 | - | 579 | 66 | 132 | 5 | 0.039 | 5 | 43.4 |
| Denmark | | 317 | 7 | .. | .. | 0.073 | 14 | 736 | 61 | 739 | 25 | 0.215 | 58 | -12.1 |
| Finland | | 284 | 16 | 149 | 9 | 0.062 | - | 346 | 31 | 181 | 25 | 0.109 | 18 | -23.4 |
| France | | 306 | 32 | 162 | - | 0.057 | - | 429 | 40 | 470 | 17 | 0.164 | 23 | -21.9 |
| Germany | | 280 | 19 | 202 | 14 | 0.086 | - | 322 | 30 | 439 | 19 | 0.180 | 13 | -29.0 |
| Greece | | 487 | 57 | .. | .. | 0.059 | - | 574 | 63 | .. | .. | 0.115 | 15 | -19.9 |
| Hungary | | 560 | 55 | 106 | - | 0.048 | - | 264 | 9 | 136 | 11 | 0.060 | 11 | 18.4 |
| Iceland | ♦ | 184 | - | n. app. | n. app. | 0.023 | - | 310 | 14 | n. app. | n. app. | 0.093 | 25 | .. |
| Ireland | | 324 | 20 | 318 | - | 0.066 | - | 421 | 27 | 473 | 11 | 0.132 | 11 | -19.8 |
| Italy | | 750 | 65 | 198 | 9 | 0.101 | 18 | 892 | 70 | 667 | 45 | 0.178 | 25 | -1.7 |
| Luxembourg | | 256 | 3 | .. | .. | .. | .. | 286 | 13 | 319 | 6 | 0.142 | 6 | -15.0 |
| Netherlands | | .. | .. | 142 | 7 | 0.071 | - | 380 | 42 | 363 | 23 | 0.148 | 24 | -7.3 |
| Norway | ♦ | 441 | 17 | n. app. | n. app. | .. | .. | 549 | 33 | n. app. | n. app. | 0.081 | 29 | 43.4 |
| Poland | | 273 | - | 138 | - | 0.040 | - | 337 | 11 | 236 | 11 | 0.067 | 13 | .. |
| Portugal | | 667 | 59 | .. | .. | 0.112 | - | 701 | 61 | .. | .. | 0.176 | 5 | -44.0 |
| Spain | | 309 | 32 | 169 | - | 0.079 | - | 359 | 42 | 613 | 15 | 0.191 | 14 | -12.2 |
| Sweden | | 249 | 16 | .. | .. | 0.045 | - | 628 | 60 | .. | .. | 0.110 | 34 | 1.9 |
| Switzerland | | 211 | 8 | 273 | 1 | 0.120 | - | 260 | 12 | 506 | 7 | 0.160 | 6 | -41.8 |
| Turkey | | .. | .. | 188 | 7 | 0.085 | 14 | 544 | 63 | 209 | 7 | 0.087 | 17 | -0.1 |
| UK | | 212 | 17 | 92 | - | 0.065 | - | 258 | 22 | 326 | 7 | 0.125 | 7 | -24.7 |

♦ See Technical Annex for data sources, notes and comments.          .. not available   - nil or negligible   n. app. not applicable

**STATE AND TRENDS SUMMARY**

Energy end-use prices influence overall energy demand and the fuel mix, which in turn largely determine environmental pressures caused by energy activities.  They can help internalise environmental costs.  Though price elasticities vary considerably by end-use sector, historical and cross-country experience suggests that the overall price effect on energy demand is strong and that increases in energy prices have reduced energy use and hence its environmental impact.

The indicators show a general downward trend in real end-use energy prices in most OECD countries, though rates of change differ greatly among countries.  Energy prices and related taxes, whether for industry or households, also vary widely among countries for all types of energy.

# TRANSPORT

*Transport is a major component of economic activity, both as a sector in itself and as a factor input to most other economic activities. It has many effects on the environment: air pollution raises concern mainly in urban areas where road traffic and congestion are concentrated, though road transport also contributes to regional and global pollution problems such as acidification and climate change; transport infrastructure leads to fragmentation of natural habitats; and vehicles entail waste management issues.*

*Road transport plays an important role in a country's environmental performance and the sustainability of its development. The volume of traffic depends on the demand for transport (largely determined by economic activity and transport prices) and on transport supply (e.g. the development of road infrastructure). Road traffic, both freight and passenger, is expected to increase further in a number of OECD countries.*

*Indicators presented here relate to:*

♦ *road traffic and vehicle intensities, i.e. traffic volumes per unit of GDP and per kilometre of road, and vehicle numbers per capita and per kilometre of road;*

♦ *road infrastructure densities, i.e. the length of road and motorway networks per square kilometre of land area;*

♦ *road fuel prices and taxes, notably the relative price and taxation levels of diesel fuel and leaded and unleaded gasoline as well as the market share of unleaded gasoline.*

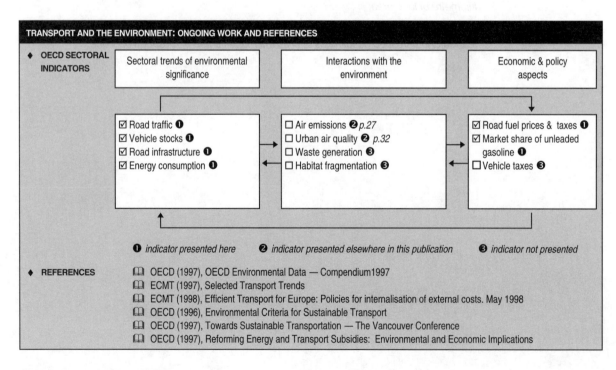

**TRANSPORT AND THE ENVIRONMENT: ONGOING WORK AND REFERENCES**

♦ **OECD SECTORAL INDICATORS**

| Sectoral trends of environmental significance | Interactions with the environment | Economic & policy aspects |
|---|---|---|
| ☑ Road traffic ❶<br>☑ Vehicle stocks ❶<br>☑ Road infrastructure ❶<br>☑ Energy consumption ❶ | ☐ Air emissions ❷ *p.27*<br>☐ Urban air quality ❷ *p.32*<br>☐ Waste generation ❸<br>☐ Habitat fragmentation ❸ | ☑ Road fuel prices & taxes ❶<br>☑ Market share of unleaded gasoline ❶<br>☐ Vehicle taxes ❸ |

❶ *indicator presented here*   ❷ *indicator presented elsewhere in this publication*   ❸ *indicator not presented*

♦ **REFERENCES**

📖 OECD (1997), OECD Environmental Data — Compendium1997
📖 ECMT (1997), Selected Transport Trends
📖 ECMT (1998), Efficient Transport for Europe: Policies for internalisation of external costs. May 1998
📖 OECD (1996), Environmental Criteria for Sustainable Transport
📖 OECD (1997), Towards Sustainable Transportation — The Vancouver Conference
📖 OECD (1997), Reforming Energy and Transport Subsidies: Environmental and Economic Implications

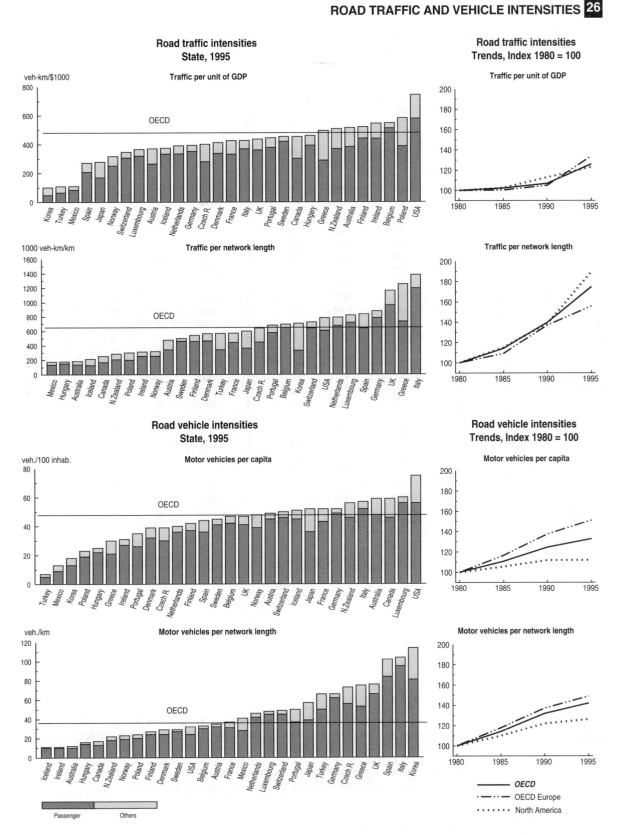

### Road traffic intensities
### State, 1995

veh-km/$1000 — Traffic per unit of GDP

### Road traffic intensities
### Trends, Index 1980 = 100

Traffic per unit of GDP

1000 veh-km/km — Traffic per network length

Traffic per network length

### Road vehicle intensities
### State, 1995

veh./100 inhab. — Motor vehicles per capita

### Road vehicle intensities
### Trends, Index 1980 = 100

Motor vehicles per capita

veh./km — Motor vehicles per network length

Motor vehicles per network length

Passenger    Others

——— OECD
—·—·— OECD Europe
·········· North America

## 26 ROAD TRAFFIC AND VEHICLE INTENSITIES

| | Road traffic | | | | | | Motor vehicles in use | | | | GDP |
| | Total volume | | Intensity | | Goods vehicles | | Total stock | | Private car ownership | | |
| | billion veh-km | % change | per unit of GDP veh-km/1 000 US$. | per network length 1 000 veh-km/km | Volume % change | share in total traffic, % | 1 000 vehicles | % change | veh./100 inh. | % change | % change |
| | 1995 | since 1980 | 1995 | 1995 | since 1980 | 1995 | 1995 | since 1980 | 1995 | since 1980 | since 1980 |
|---|---|---|---|---|---|---|---|---|---|---|---|
| Canada | 260 | 27 | 454 | 255 | 65 | 33 | 17524 | 33 | 46 | 11 | 43 |
| Mexico | 55 | 29 | 110 | 179 | 1 | 24 | 12485 | 102 | 9 | 34 | 29 |
| USA ♦ | 4890 | 102 | 745 | 784 | 75 | 22 | 197639 | 27 | 56 | 6 | 46 |
| Japan ♦ | 687 | 77 | 281 | 600 | 86 | 38 | 65353 | 76 | 36 | 76 | 59 |
| Korea | 53 | 504 | 101 | 708 | 586 | 46 | 8469 | 1505 | 13 | 1939 | 241 |
| Australia ♦ | 167 | 45 | 515 | 186 | 55 | 24 | 10651 | 47 | 48 | 21 | 57 |
| N.Zealand | 26 | 60 | 508 | 288 | 89 | 25 | 2008 | 28 | 46 | 10 | 41 |
| Austria | 54 | 52 | 371 | 479 | 61 | 27 | 3906 | 60 | 45 | 50 | 37 |
| Belgium ♦ | 99 | 116 | 548 | 694 | 34 | 6 | 4699 | 35 | 42 | 30 | 28 |
| Czech R. | 36 | 71 | 402 | 641 | 9 | 10 | 4069 | 50 | 30 | 76 | .. |
| Denmark | 41 | 54 | 414 | 567 | 62 | 17 | 2027 | 23 | 32 | 19 | 35 |
| Finland | 42 | 58 | 522 | 543 | 48 | 14 | 2161 | 56 | 37 | 45 | 32 |
| France ♦ | 464 | 57 | 427 | 571 | 81 | 21 | 30295 | 40 | 43 | 22 | 33 |
| Germany ♦ | 569 | .. | 395 | 879 | .. | 10 | 42743 | .. | 49 | .. | .. |
| w.Germany ♦ | 500 | 50 | 383 | 957 | 51 | 10 | 35207 | 44 | 51 | 35 | 36 |
| Greece ♦ | 51 | 151 | 495 | 1253 | 122 | 37 | 3076 | 143 | 21 | 134 | 24 |
| Hungary | 28 | 49 | 461 | 179 | -39 | 12 | 2603 | 121 | 22 | 136 | .. |
| Iceland ♦ | 2 | 97 | 375 | 216 | 73 | 8 | 135 | 41 | 45 | 18 | 36 |
| Ireland | 29 | 57 | 546 | 315 | 49 | 18 | 1082 | 35 | 27 | 23 | 84 |
| Italy ♦ | 435 | 92 | 427 | 1383 | 63 | 12 | 32807 | 72 | 52 | 67 | 32 |
| Luxembourg ♦ | 4 | 90 | 367 | 821 | 153 | 11 | 249 | 74 | 56 | 54 | 100 |
| Netherlands ♦ | 105 | 50 | 391 | 790 | 75 | 14 | 6223 | 37 | 36 | 22 | 38 |
| Norway | 29 | 53 | 318 | 321 | 103 | 14 | 2067 | 48 | 39 | 28 | 52 |
| Poland | 113 | 153 | 583 | 303 | 60 | 29 | 8956 | 192 | 19 | 191 | .. |
| Portugal | 47 | 118 | 446 | 682 | 53 | 14 | 3439 | 185 | 26 | 169 | 43 |
| Spain ♦ | 141 | 100 | 272 | 838 | 88 | 22 | 17196 | 92 | 36 | 79 | 44 |
| Sweden ♦ | 68 | 53 | 454 | 499 | 67 | 6 | 3953 | 28 | 41 | 18 | 24 |
| Switzerland ♦ | 51 | 43 | 348 | 724 | 48 | 11 | 3507 | 44 | 46 | 30 | 23 |
| Turkey ♦ | 35 | 136 | 109 | 569 | 89 | 32 | 4041 | 245 | 5 | 197 | 94 |
| UK ♦ | 427 | 77 | 437 | 1163 | 67 | 16 | 27942 | 61 | 41 | 51 | 38 |
| OECD | 9008 | 85 | 497 | 653 | 73 | 22 | 521305 | 50 | 38 | 31 | .. |

♦ See Technical Annex for data sources, notes and comments.

**STATE AND TRENDS
SUMMARY**

From 1980, countries' efforts in introducing cleaner vehicles have largely been offset by growth in vehicle stocks and the rapid increase of their use. In most OECD countries road traffic growth rates exceeded economic growth.

Traffic intensities per unit of GDP and per length of network show wide variations among OECD countries. The same holds for vehicle availability per capita and vehicle density.

## ROAD INFRASTRUCTURE DENSITIES 27

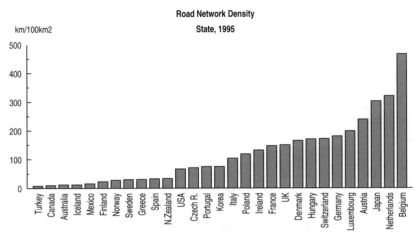

**Road Network Density**
State, 1995

km/100km2

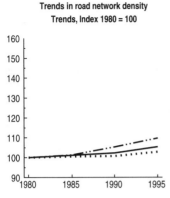

**Trends in road network density**
Trends, Index 1980 = 100

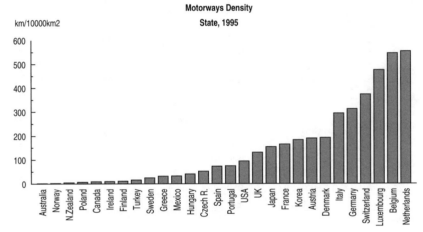

**Motorways Density**
State, 1995

km/10000km2

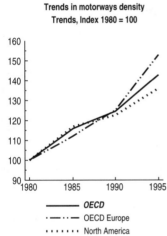

**Trends in motorways density**
Trends, Index 1980 = 100

—— OECD
—·—·— OECD Europe
········ North America

## 27 ROAD INFRASTRUCTURE DENSITIES

| | | Road network | | | Motorways | | | GDP |
|---|---|---|---|---|---|---|---|---|
| | | Total length | | Density | Total length | | Density | |
| | | 1 000 km 1995 | % change since 1980 | km/100 km² 1995 | km 1995 | % change since 1980 | km/10 000 km² 1995 | % change since 1980 |
| Canada | | 1021 | 12 | 10 | 9649 | 105 | 10 | 43 |
| Mexico | ♦ | 308 | 44 | 16 | 6368 | 583 | 33 | 29 |
| USA | | 6239 | 0 | 67 | 88500 | 24 | 95 | 46 |
| Japan | | 1144 | 3 | 303 | 5860 | 127 | 155 | 59 |
| Korea | | 74 | 58 | 75 | 1824 | 49 | 184 | 241 |
| Australia | ♦ | 895 | 10 | 12 | 1330 | 22 | 2 | 57 |
| N.Zealand | | 92 | -1 | 34 | 144 | 21 | 5 | 41 |
| Austria | ♦ | 200 | .. | 239 | 1596 | 70 | 190 | 37 |
| Belgium | | 143 | 12 | 467 | 1666 | 40 | 546 | 28 |
| Czech R. | | 56 | 0 | 71 | 414 | 60 | 52 | .. |
| Denmark | | 71 | 4 | 166 | 830 | 61 | 193 | 35 |
| Finland | ♦ | 78 | 4 | 23 | 388 | 100 | 11 | 32 |
| France | ♦ | 813 | 1 | 147 | 9140 | 74 | 166 | 33 |
| Germany | | 648 | .. | 181 | 11143 | .. | 312 | .. |
| w.Germany | | 523 | 9 | 210 | 9297 | 27 | 374 | 36 |
| Greece | ♦ | 41 | 10 | 31 | 420 | 362 | 32 | 24 |
| Hungary | | 159 | 81 | 171 | 378 | 81 | 41 | .. |
| Iceland | | 12 | -1 | 12 | - | - | - | 36 |
| Ireland | | 92 | 0 | 132 | 70 | .. | 10 | 84 |
| Italy | | 314 | 6 | 104 | 8860 | 50 | 294 | 32 |
| Luxembourg | | 5 | 1 | 199 | 123 | 180 | 476 | 100 |
| Netherlands | | 133 | 23 | 321 | 2300 | 30 | 554 | 38 |
| Norway | | 90 | 10 | 28 | 86 | 51 | 3 | 52 |
| Poland | | 372 | 25 | 119 | 246 | 77 | 8 | .. |
| Portugal | | 69 | 32 | 75 | 687 | 441 | 75 | 43 |
| Spain | ♦ | 168 | 11 | 33 | 3692 | 100 | 73 | 44 |
| Sweden | ♦ | 136 | 6 | 30 | 1141 | 34 | 25 | 24 |
| Switzerland | | 71 | 7 | 172 | 1540 | 32 | 373 | 23 |
| Turkey | ♦ | 61 | 2 | 8 | 1246 | 5092 | 16 | 94 |
| UK | ♦ | 367 | 8 | 150 | 3200 | 24 | 131 | 38 |
| OECD | | 13786 | 5 | 40 | 162841 | 43 | 47 | .. |

♦ See Technical Annex for data sources, notes and comments.

**STATE AND TRENDS**     Length of road network is an indicator of transport infrastructure development, which in turn is an important component of transport supply. Transport infrastructure exerts pressures on the environment through use of space and physical transformation of the natural environment (e.g. fragmentation of habitats).

Density of road infrastructure varies greatly among OECD countries (from 1 to 50). The length of motorways often grows faster than GDP.

## ROAD FUEL PRICES AND TAXES 28

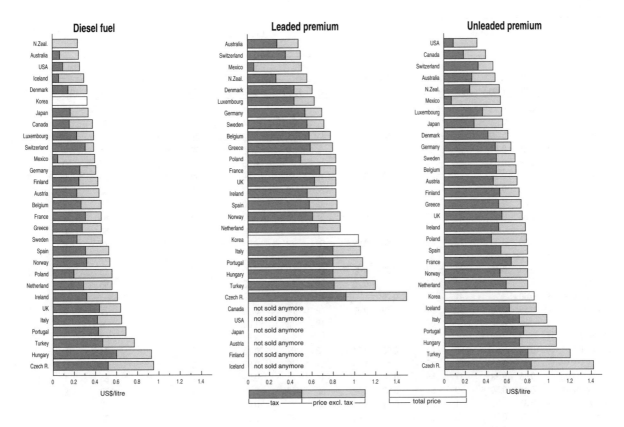

## 28 ROAD FUEL PRICES AND TAXES

| | Diesel | | | | Leaded premium | | | | Unleaded gasoline | | Market share of unleaded | Energy consumption by road transport | | |
|---|---|---|---|---|---|---|---|---|---|---|---|---|---|---|
| | Price US$/litre | | Taxation % of price | | Price US$/litre | | Taxation % of price | | Price US$/litre | Taxation % of price | gasoline % | share of total cons. | Total Mtoe | % change since |
| | 1980 | 1995 | 1980 | 1995 | 1980 | 1995 | 1980 | 1995 | 1995 | 1995 | 1995 | 1995 | 1995 | 1980 |
| Canada ♦ | 0.52 | 0.38 | .. | 41 | .. | .. | .. | .. | 0.41 | 47 | 100 | 73 | 36 | 3 |
| Mexico ♦ | .. | 0.39 | .. | 12 | .. | 0.52 | .. | 12 | 0.54 | 12 | .. | 91 | 32 | 111 |
| USA ♦ | 0.44 | 0.26 | 15 | 40 | 0.54 | .. | .. | .. | 0.32 | 29 | 100 | 80 | 436 | 26 |
| Japan ♦ | 0.65 | 0.34 | 24 | 51 | .. | .. | .. | .. | 0.56 | 52 | 100 | 82 | 71 | 63 |
| Korea ♦ | 0.96 | 0.33 | .. | .. | 3.79 | 1.04 | .. | .. | 0.86 | .. | .. | 77 | 20 | 1859 |
| Australia ♦ | .. | 0.25 | .. | 27 | 0.47 | 0.49 | 19 | 58 | 0.49 | 58 | 58 | 80 | 20 | 43 |
| N.Zealand ♦ | 0.65 | 0.24 | 2 | 1 | 0.83 | 0.56 | 28 | 48 | 0.53 | 48 | 44 | 52 | 2 | 37 |
| Austria | 0.85 | 0.44 | 33 | 52 | 0.93 | .. | 42 | .. | 0.70 | 67 | 100 | 86 | 5 | 33 |
| Belgium | 0.52 | 0.45 | 34 | 59 | 0.94 | 0.77 | 53 | 75 | 0.70 | 72 | 30 | 83 | 7 | 43 |
| Czech R. | .. | 0.95 | .. | 55 | .. | 1.49 | .. | 62 | 1.42 | 58 | 47 | 85 | 2 | 18 |
| Denmark ♦ | 0.36 | 0.33 | 0 | 47 | 0.88 | 0.62 | 59 | 72 | 0.61 | 69 | 90 | 76 | 4 | 53 |
| Finland ♦ | .. | 0.43 | .. | 58 | 0.92 | .. | 36 | .. | 0.72 | 74 | 50 | 85 | 4 | 40 |
| France ♦ | 0.68 | 0.46 | 47 | 67 | 0.98 | 0.83 | 58 | 82 | 0.80 | 80 | 41 | 85 | 40 | 41 |
| Germany | .. | 0.41 | .. | 64 | .. | 0.70 | .. | 77 | 0.65 | 76 | 85 | 86 | 55 | 36 |
| w.Germany ♦ | 0.66 | .. | 41 | .. | 0.76 | .. | 49 | .. | .. | .. | .. | .. | .. | .. |
| Greece | 0.59 | 0.46 | 13 | 61 | 1.39 | 0.80 | 42 | 74 | 0.74 | 70 | 23 | 71 | 5 | 100 |
| Hungary | .. | 0.92 | .. | 65 | .. | 1.12 | 18 | 72 | 1.08 | 67 | .. | 86 | 2 | 21 |
| Iceland ♦ | .. | 0.30 | .. | 20 | .. | .. | .. | .. | 0.88 | 70 | 87 | 67 | 0 | 54 |
| Ireland | 0.69 | 0.61 | 28 | 53 | 0.96 | 0.84 | 48 | 67 | 0.78 | 66 | 25 | 74 | 2 | 29 |
| Italy | 0.55 | 0.65 | 8 | 65 | 1.40 | 1.05 | 61 | 76 | 0.99 | 73 | .. | 89 | 35 | 56 |
| Luxembourg | 0.45 | 0.39 | 17 | 58 | 0.70 | 0.63 | 44 | 71 | 0.56 | 67 | .. | 85 | 1 | 166 |
| Netherlands | 0.47 | 0.56 | 23 | 51 | 0.82 | 0.87 | 52 | 76 | 0.80 | 74 | 75 | 72 | 9 | 31 |
| Norway ♦ | 0.31 | 0.55 | 1 | 59 | 0.71 | 0.86 | 52 | 70 | 0.80 | 66 | 43 | 67 | 3 | 50 |
| Poland | .. | 0.55 | .. | 36 | .. | 0.83 | .. | 60 | 0.80 | 57 | .. | 85 | 8 | 5 |
| Portugal | 0.83 | 0.69 | 7 | 62 | 2.22 | 1.08 | 61 | 74 | 1.07 | 71 | 2 | 84 | 4 | 116 |
| Spain | 0.64 | 0.52 | 25 | 59 | 1.28 | 0.84 | 35 | 69 | 0.79 | 68 | 2 | 78 | 21 | 96 |
| Sweden | 0.33 | 0.46 | 8 | 49 | 0.67 | 0.72 | 49 | 78 | 0.68 | 73 | 100 | 84 | 7 | 26 |
| Switzerland ♦ | 0.85 | 0.40 | 51 | 79 | 0.82 | 0.50 | 51 | 73 | 0.47 | 71 | 77 | 75 | 5 | 41 |
| Turkey | 0.88 | 0.78 | .. | 61 | 1.50 | 1.20 | .. | 68 | 1.20 | 67 | 2 | 86 | 10 | 115 |
| UK | 0.76 | 0.64 | 40 | 68 | 0.87 | 0.83 | 46 | 76 | 0.75 | 74 | 57 | 78 | 37 | 41 |

♦ *See Technical Annex for data sources, notes and comments.*

**STATE AND TRENDS SUMMARY**

Prices are a key form of information for consumers. When fuel prices rise relative to other goods, this tends to reduce demand for fuels and stimulate energy saving, and may influence the fuel structure of energy consumption. Road fuel prices vary from 1 to three in OECD countries.

The use of taxation to influence energy consumer behaviour and to internalise environmental costs is increasing. Taxation of unleaded fuel ranges from 12 to 80 per cent of the price. Many OECD countries have introduced tax differentials in favour of unleaded gasoline and some have imposed environmental taxes (e.g. relating to sulphur content) on energy products.

# AGRICULTURE

*The economic and social significance of the agricultural sector has been declining in most OECD countries for decades. Agriculture's environmental effects can be negative or positive. They depend on the scale, type and intensity of farming as well as on agro-ecological and physical factors and on climate and weather. Farming can lead to deterioration in soil, water and air quality, and to loss of natural habitats and biodiversity. These environmental changes can have important implications for the level of agricultural production and food supply, and can limit the <u>sustainable development</u> of agriculture. But farming can also provide sinks for greenhouse gases, conserve biodiversity and landscapes and help prevent floods and landslides.*

*The main environmental concerns related to agriculture include nitrogen and phosphorus run-off from excessive commercial fertiliser use, intensive livestock farming and pesticides. Nitrogen and phosphorus, while major plant nutrients, are responsible for water eutrophication and related effects on aquatic life and water quality. Pesticide use adds persistent organic chemicals to ecosystems; these tend to accumulate in the soil and in biota, and residues may leach into surface and groundwaters. The general population can be exposed to pesticides through food.*

*<u>Indicators</u> presented here relate to:*

♦ *<u>intensity of use of nitrogen and phosphate fertilisers</u> in agriculture, reflected through apparent consumption in tonnes of active ingredients (N and P per $km^2$ of agricultural land). This represents potential pressure on the environment in the absence of effective pollution abatement. These indicators could be extended to include nitrogen and phosphate emissions from all point and non-point sources, corrected for absorption of phosphates and nitrogen by crops. This could further lead to the establishment of a proper nutrient balance.*

♦ *<u>livestock densities</u>, reflected through the number of head of cattle, pigs, sheep and goats per $km^2$ of agricultural land; the amount of N and P generated by livestock manure per $km^2$ of agricultural land is provided to complete the picture.*

♦ *<u>intensity of use of pesticides</u> in agriculture, reflected through apparent consumption or sales expressed in tonnes of active ingredients per $km^2$ of agricultural land. This indicator does not recognise differences among pesticides in levels of toxicity, persistence and mobility. It can be considered a first step towards a more comprehensive indicator based on an internationally agreed list of substances with appropriate weighting factors. Using $km^2$ of land where pesticides are actually applied as the denominator would provide important complementary information about intensity of pesticide use.*

*It should be noted that these indicators describe potential environmental pressures, and may hide important sub-national variations. Indicators of livestock densities are first approximations of potential environmental pressure; more information is needed to describe the actual pressure.*

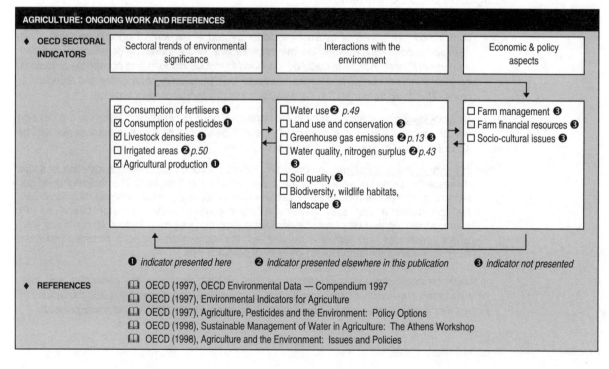

**AGRICULTURE: ONGOING WORK AND REFERENCES**

◆ **OECD SECTORAL INDICATORS**

| Sectoral trends of environmental significance | Interactions with the environment | Economic & policy aspects |
|---|---|---|

**Sectoral trends of environmental significance**
- ☑ Consumption of fertilisers ❶
- ☑ Consumption of pesticides ❶
- ☑ Livestock densities ❶
- ☐ Irrigated areas ❷ *p.50*
- ☑ Agricultural production ❶

**Interactions with the environment**
- ☐ Water use ❷ *p.49*
- ☐ Land use and conservation ❸
- ☐ Greenhouse gas emissions ❷ *p.13* ❸
- ☐ Water quality, nitrogen surplus ❷ *p.43* ❸
- ☐ Soil quality ❸
- ☐ Biodiversity, wildlife habitats, landscape ❸

**Economic & policy aspects**
- ☐ Farm management ❸
- ☐ Farm financial resources ❸
- ☐ Socio-cultural issues ❸

❶ *indicator presented here*   ❷ *indicator presented elsewhere in this publication*   ❸ *indicator not presented*

◆ **REFERENCES**
- 📖 OECD (1997), OECD Environmental Data — Compendium 1997
- 📖 OECD (1997), Environmental Indicators for Agriculture
- 📖 OECD (1997), Agriculture, Pesticides and the Environment: Policy Options
- 📖 OECD (1998), Sustainable Management of Water in Agriculture: The Athens Workshop
- 📖 OECD (1998), Agriculture and the Environment: Issues and Policies

# INTENSITY OF USE OF NITROGEN AND PHOSPHATE FERTILISERS 29

### Nitrogen from fertilizers per km2 of agricultural land

Trends (tonnes/km2)          % change 1980-95

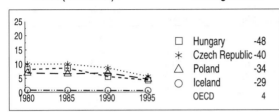

| | | |
|---|---|---|
| □ | Hungary | -48 |
| ✳ | Czech Republic | -40 |
| △ | Poland | -34 |
| ○ | Iceland | -29 |
| | OECD | 4 |

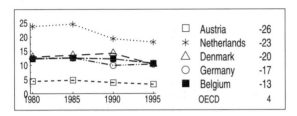

| | | |
|---|---|---|
| □ | Austria | -26 |
| ✳ | Netherlands | -23 |
| △ | Denmark | -20 |
| ○ | Germany | -17 |
| ■ | Belgium | -13 |
| | OECD | 4 |

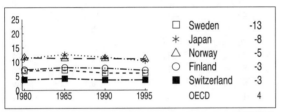

| | | |
|---|---|---|
| □ | Sweden | -13 |
| ✳ | Japan | -8 |
| △ | Norway | -5 |
| ○ | Finland | -3 |
| ■ | Switzerland | -3 |
| | OECD | 4 |

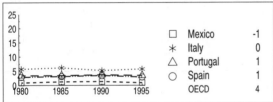

| | | |
|---|---|---|
| □ | Mexico | -1 |
| ✳ | Italy | 0 |
| △ | Portugal | 1 |
| ○ | Spain | 1 |
| | OECD | 4 |

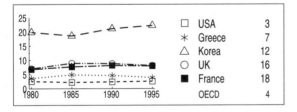

| | | |
|---|---|---|
| □ | USA | 3 |
| ✳ | Greece | 7 |
| △ | Korea | 12 |
| ○ | UK | 16 |
| ■ | France | 18 |
| | OECD | 4 |

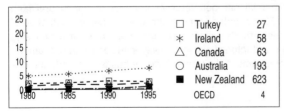

| | | |
|---|---|---|
| □ | Turkey | 27 |
| ✳ | Ireland | 58 |
| △ | Canada | 63 |
| ○ | Australia | 193 |
| ■ | New Zealand | 623 |
| | OECD | 4 |

### Phosphate from fertilizers per km2 of agricultural land

Trends (tonnes/km2)          % change 1980-95

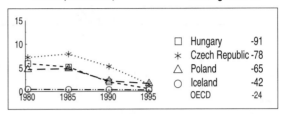

| | | |
|---|---|---|
| □ | Hungary | -91 |
| ✳ | Czech Republic | -78 |
| △ | Poland | -65 |
| ○ | Iceland | -42 |
| | OECD | -24 |

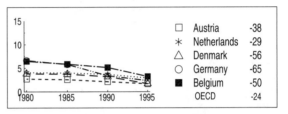

| | | |
|---|---|---|
| □ | Austria | -38 |
| ✳ | Netherlands | -29 |
| △ | Denmark | -56 |
| ○ | Germany | -65 |
| ■ | Belgium | -50 |
| | OECD | -24 |

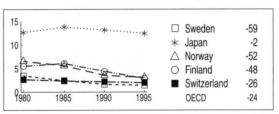

| | | |
|---|---|---|
| □ | Sweden | -59 |
| ✳ | Japan | -2 |
| △ | Norway | -52 |
| ○ | Finland | -48 |
| ■ | Switzerland | -26 |
| | OECD | -24 |

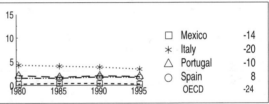

| | | |
|---|---|---|
| □ | Mexico | -14 |
| ✳ | Italy | -20 |
| △ | Portugal | -10 |
| ○ | Spain | 8 |
| | OECD | -24 |

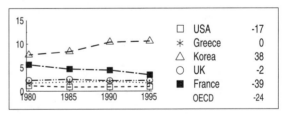

| | | |
|---|---|---|
| □ | USA | -17 |
| ✳ | Greece | 0 |
| △ | Korea | 38 |
| ○ | UK | -2 |
| ■ | France | -39 |
| | OECD | -24 |

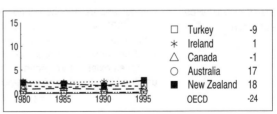

| | | |
|---|---|---|
| □ | Turkey | -9 |
| ✳ | Ireland | 1 |
| △ | Canada | -1 |
| ○ | Australia | 17 |
| ■ | New Zealand | 18 |
| | OECD | -24 |

## 29 INTENSITY OF USE OF NITROGEN AND PHOSPHATE FERTILISERS

| | | Intensity of use of commercial nitrogen and phosphate fertilizers apparent consumption per km² of agricultural land | | | | Agricultural production | | Agricultural value added |
|---|---|---|---|---|---|---|---|---|
| | | Nitrogen | | Phosphate | | Crops | Total | |
| | | tonnes/km² 1995 | % change since 1980 | tonnes/km² 1995 | % change since 1980 | % change since 1980 | % change since 1980 | % GDP 1995 |
| Canada | | 2.2 | 63 | 0.9 | -1 | 50.5 | 39.2 | 2.1 |
| Mexico | ◆ | 0.9 | -1 | 0.2 | -14 | 16.9 | 34.7 | 5.0 |
| USA | ◆ | 2.6 | 3 | 1.0 | -17 | 14.4 | 20.9 | 1.8 |
| Japan | | 10.4 | -8 | 12.4 | -2 | -9.0 | 3.6 | 1.9 |
| Korea | ◆ | 22.3 | 12 | 10.6 | 38 | 31.8 | 55.0 | 6.5 |
| Australia | | 0.1 | 193 | 0.2 | 17 | 84.9 | 36.0 | 3.4 |
| N.Zealand | | 1.0 | 623 | 2.7 | 18 | 65.3 | 17.6 | 8.3 |
| Austria | | 3.2 | -26 | 1.7 | -38 | -3.5 | 7.7 | 1.5 |
| Belgium | ◆ | 10.6 | -13 | 3.2 | -50 | 48.1 | 30.7 | 1.3 |
| Czech Rep. | | 5.9 | -40 | 1.6 | -78 | -6.5 | -13.0 | 4.1 |
| Denmark | ◆ | 10.3 | -20 | 1.7 | -56 | 43.4 | 22.0 | 3.6 |
| Finland | | 7.0 | -3 | 2.8 | -48 | 9.0 | -4.3 | 3.7 |
| France | ◆ | 8.0 | 18 | 3.4 | -39 | 10.5 | 6.0 | 2.4 |
| Germany | ◆ | 10.3 | -17 | 2.3 | -65 | 13.2 | -2.0 | *1.0* |
| Greece | ◆ | 3.9 | 7 | 1.7 | - | 15.7 | 13.8 | 12.0 |
| Hungary | ◆ | 4.2 | -48 | 0.5 | -91 | -25.2 | -25.9 | 7.2 |
| Iceland | ◆ | 0.6 | -29 | 0.3 | -42 | -41.1 | -17.9 | 8.9 |
| Ireland | | 7.6 | 58 | 2.5 | 1 | 7.8 | 16.8 | 5.7 |
| Italy | | 5.7 | - | 3.4 | -20 | -10.9 | -4.3 | 2.9 |
| Netherlands | | 18.1 | -23 | 2.9 | -29 | 38.8 | 18.9 | 3.1 |
| Norway | | 11.0 | -5 | 3.1 | -52 | -1.8 | 6.7 | 2.5 |
| Poland | ◆ | 4.6 | -34 | 1.6 | -65 | 34.0 | 0.1 | 7.6 |
| Portugal | | 3.5 | 1 | 1.8 | -10 | 8.6 | 36.6 | 3.7 |
| Spain | ◆ | 2.9 | 1 | 1.6 | 8 | -14.3 | 0.5 | 2.9 |
| Sweden | ◆ | 6.0 | -13 | 1.4 | -59 | -3.3 | -3.8 | 2.0 |
| Switzerland | | 3.6 | -3 | 2.0 | -26 | 2.7 | 1.2 | 3.0 |
| Turkey | ◆ | 2.7 | 27 | 1.5 | -9 | 37.3 | 36.2 | 15.7 |
| UK | ◆ | 8.1 | 16 | 2.2 | -2 | 18.7 | 10.0 | 1.7 |
| OECD | ◆ | 2.1 | 4 | 0.9 | -24 | .. | .. | *2.6* |

◆ *See Technical Annex for data sources, notes and comments.*

**STATE AND TRENDS SUMMARY**

Overall apparent consumption of commercial nitrogen fertiliser per unit of agricultural land since 1980 has grown in a number of OECD countries, and in the world, while consumption of phosphate fertiliser has decreased. These trends reflect developments aimed at maximising yield per hectare through specialisation and intensification. However major variations among countries exist. More recently the use of commercial nitrogen fertiliser has levelled off, and has declined in a number of countries.

## LIVESTOCK DENSITIES 30

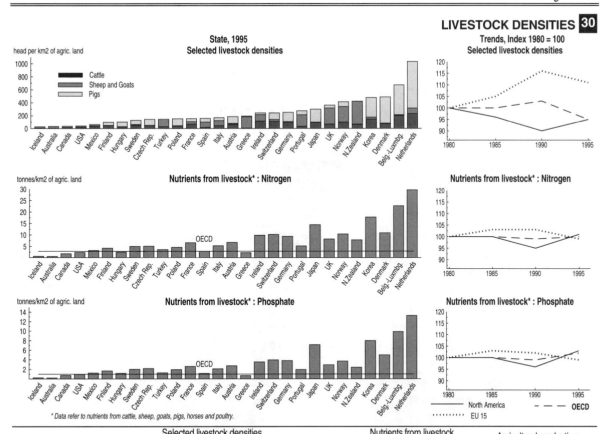

State, 1995
Selected livestock densities

Trends, Index 1980 = 100
Selected livestock densities

Nutrients from livestock* : Nitrogen

Nutrients from livestock* : Nitrogen

Nutrients from livestock* : Phosphate

Nutrients from livestock* : Phosphate

head per km2 of agric. land

tonnes/km2 of agric. land

Cattle
Sheep and Goats
Pigs

OECD

North America — — — OECD
·········· EU 15

* Data refer to nutrients from cattle, sheep, goats, pigs, horses and poultry.

|  | Selected livestock densities per km² of agricultural land | | | | | | Nutrients from livestock per km² of agricultural land | | Agricultural production | |
|---|---|---|---|---|---|---|---|---|---|---|
|  | Cattle | | Sheep and Goats | | Pigs | | Nitrogen | Phosphate | Livestock prod. | Total |
|  | head/km² 1995 | % change 1980-95 | head/km² 1995 | % change 1980-95 | head/km² 1995 | % change 1980-95 | tonnes/km² 1995 | tonnes/km² 1995 | % change 1980-95 | % change 1980-95 |
| Canada | 19.0 | 7 | 1.0 | 29 | 17.2 | 17 | 1.8 | 0.7 | 23.4 | 39.2 |
| Mexico | 30.4 | 9 | 16.6 | 2 | 16.0 | -6 | 3.2 | 1.2 | 52.8 | 34.7 |
| USA | 24.1 | -7 | 2.5 | -24 | 14.1 | -11 | 2.3 | 1.0 | 25.8 | 20.9 |
| Japan | 96.7 | 24 | 1.1 | -24 | 201.7 | 10 | 14.4 | 7.1 | 14.4 | 3.6 |
| Korea | 146.7 | 102 | 30.3 | 230 | 301.2 | 279 | 17.7 | 8.0 | 165.6 | 55.0 |
| Australia | 5.6 | 5 | 26.7 | -3 | 0.6 | 13 | 0.6 | 0.2 | 20.8 | 36.0 |
| N.Zealand | 66.6 | 20 | 352.9 | -25 | 3.1 | 4 | 7.8 | 2.4 | 15.0 | 17.6 |
| Austria | 67.1 | -3 | 12.1 | 93 | 106.9 | -2 | 6.7 | 2.7 | 11.9 | 7.7 |
| Belgium ♦ | 203.3 | 4 | 10.9 | 51 | 460.2 | 44 | 22.7 | 9.9 | 28.3 | 30.7 |
| Czech Rep. ♦ | 46.5 | -43 | 3.1 | -56 | 93.8 | -20 | 5.1 | 2.2 | -18.0 | -13.0 |
| Denmark | 76.7 | -25 | 5.3 | 176 | 406.6 | 19 | 10.8 | 5.0 | 15.3 | 22.0 |
| Finland | 45.2 | -30 | 3.2 | -18 | 49.4 | -7 | 4.2 | 1.7 | -14.6 | -4.3 |
| France | 68.3 | -9 | 37.9 | -8 | 48.5 | 35 | 6.6 | 2.6 | 6.4 | 6.0 |
| Germany | 92.6 | -17 | 14.5 | -16 | 143.9 | -23 | 9.3 | 3.8 | -14.7 | -2.0 |
| Greece | 6.9 | -32 | 176.6 | 29 | 10.9 | 5 | 2.2 | 0.7 | -1.0 | 13.8 |
| Hungary | 14.7 | -49 | 16.2 | -64 | 70.5 | -44 | 2.5 | 1.2 | -28.6 | -25.9 |
| Iceland | 3.9 | 22 | 24.1 | -45 | 0.2 | 140 | 0.7 | 0.2 | -17.0 | -17.9 |
| Ireland | 114.2 | 6 | 102.8 | 150 | 26.7 | 36 | 9.8 | 3.5 | 16.5 | 16.8 |
| Italy | 44.7 | -10 | 75.7 | 32 | 50.1 | 0 | 5.2 | 2.1 | 9.1 | -4.3 |
| Netherlands | 231.3 | -10 | 85.7 | 96 | 715.7 | 44 | 29.7 | 13.3 | 13.3 | 18.9 |
| Norway | 97.3 | -6 | 242.5 | 11 | 74.9 | 8 | 10.4 | 3.7 | 7.8 | 6.7 |
| Poland | 39.1 | -41 | 3.8 | -83 | 109.4 | -2 | 4.5 | 1.9 | -21.6 | 0.1 |
| Portugal | 34.1 | 2 | 179.5 | 35 | 61.6 | -30 | 5.1 | 1.9 | 49.5 | 36.6 |
| Spain | 17.9 | 19 | 83.1 | 56 | 58.9 | 72 | 2.9 | 1.1 | 25.6 | 0.5 |
| Sweden | 49.9 | -8 | 12.9 | 18 | 64.9 | -15 | 5.0 | 2.0 | -2.6 | -3.8 |
| Switzerland | 111.1 | -3 | 30.9 | 26 | 101.9 | -18 | 10.2 | 3.9 | -3.1 | 1.2 |
| Turkey | 30.3 | -25 | 115.3 | -32 | 0.0 | -40 | 3.6 | 1.3 | 27.3 | 36.2 |
| UK | 68.4 | -9 | 249.3 | 105 | 43.9 | 0 | 8.1 | 2.9 | 4.6 | 10.0 |
| OECD | 23.0 | .. | 29.1 | .. | 19.8 | .. | 2.5 | 1.0 | .. | .. |

♦ *See Technical Annex for data sources, notes and comments.*

# 31 INTENSITY OF USE OF PESTICIDES

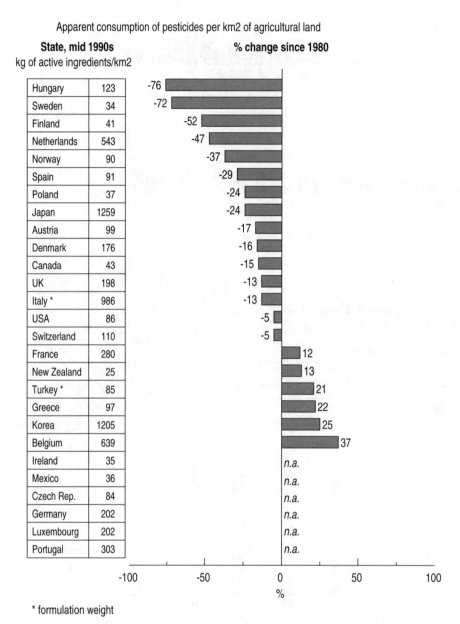

Apparent consumption of pesticides per km2 of agricultural land

**State, mid 1990s**
kg of active ingredients/km2

**% change since 1980**

| Country | kg/km2 | % change |
|---|---|---|
| Hungary | 123 | -76 |
| Sweden | 34 | -72 |
| Finland | 41 | -52 |
| Netherlands | 543 | -47 |
| Norway | 90 | -37 |
| Spain | 91 | -29 |
| Poland | 37 | -24 |
| Japan | 1259 | -24 |
| Austria | 99 | -17 |
| Denmark | 176 | -16 |
| Canada | 43 | -15 |
| UK | 198 | -13 |
| Italy * | 986 | -13 |
| USA | 86 | -5 |
| Switzerland | 110 | -5 |
| France | 280 | 12 |
| New Zealand | 25 | 13 |
| Turkey * | 85 | 21 |
| Greece | 97 | 22 |
| Korea | 1205 | 25 |
| Belgium | 639 | 37 |
| Ireland | 35 | n.a. |
| Mexico | 36 | n.a. |
| Czech Rep. | 84 | n.a. |
| Germany | 202 | n.a. |
| Luxembourg | 202 | n.a. |
| Portugal | 303 | n.a. |

* formulation weight

**STATE AND TRENDS SUMMARY**
The intensity of use of pesticides i.e. the apparent consumption of pesticides per km$^2$ of agricultural land has declined in a number of OECD countries since 1980, though major variations exist among countries. This indicator describes potential pressure on the environment; it does not recognise differences among pesticides in levels of toxicity, persistence and mobility.

# EXPENDITURE

*Efforts to reduce environmental pressures imply public and private expenditure, to: i) finance pollution abatement and control at national level, and ii) provide financial and technical support for environmental protection measures in developing countries.*

*Indicators presented here relate to:*

♦ *levels of <u>pollution abatement and control (PAC) expenditure</u> as a general indication of how much a country spends on controlling and reducing pressures from pollution. This expenditure is disaggregated by medium (air, water, waste) and by the sector undertaking the measures (public sector, businesses, households). Activities such as nature protection, natural resource preservation and water supply are excluded, as is expenditure on workplace protection, energy saving or improvement of production processes for commercial or technical reasons, though these may have environmental benefits.*

♦ *levels of <u>official development assistance</u> (ODA), as part of ODA supports sustainable development and, in particular, environmental protection.*

**EXPENDITURE: REFERENCES**

  📖 OECD (1997), OECD Environmental Data — Compendium 1997
  📖 OECD (1996), Pollution abatement and control expenditure in OECD countries
  📖 OECD (1998), Pollution abatement and control expenditure in OECD countrie s, forthcoming

## POLLUTION ABATEMENT AND CONTROL EXPENDITURE 32

**OECD PAC expenditure, mid-1990s**

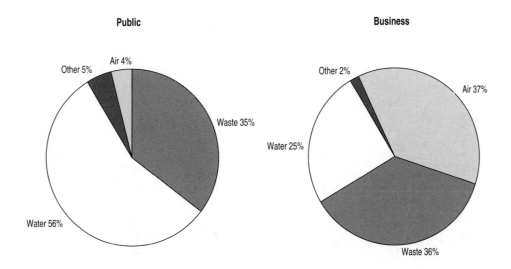

Public

Business

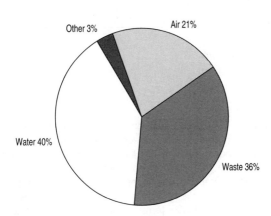

Total *

* excluding households; based on data for 10 countries representing 70 per cent of the GDP of the OECD.

## 32 POLLUTION ABATEMENT AND CONTROL EXPENDITURE

| | | PAC expenditure, mid-1990s or latest available year | | | | | |
|---|---|---|---|---|---|---|---|
| | | as % of GDP | | | in US$ per capita | | |
| | | Public | Business | Total* | Public | Business | Total* |
| Canada | ◆ | 0.7 | 0.5 | 1.2 | 143 | 95 | 238 |
| Mexico | ◆ | 0.3 | .. | .. | 25 | .. | .. |
| USA | ◆ | 0.7 | 0.9 | 1.6 | 177 | 246 | 422 |
| Japan | ◆ | 0.9 | 0.6 | 1.6 | 168 | 115 | 283 |
| Korea | ◆ | 0.8 | 0.7 | 1.6 | 104 | 92 | 196 |
| Australia | ◆ | 0.5 | 0.3 | 0.8 | 94 | 54 | 149 |
| Austria | ◆ | 1.2 | 0.9 | 2.1 | 232 | 158 | 391 |
| Belgium | ◆ | 0.4 | .. | .. | 75 | .. | .. |
| Denmark | ◆ | 0.7 | .. | .. | 161 | .. | .. |
| Finland | ◆ | 0.6 | 0.5 | 1.1 | 97 | 78 | 175 |
| France | ◆ | 0.9 | 0.5 | 1.4 | 188 | 93 | 281 |
| Germany | ◆ | 0.8 | 0.6 | 1.4 | 171 | 136 | 307 |
| Greece | ◆ | 0.2 | .. | .. | 17 | .. | .. |
| Hungary | ◆ | .. | .. | 0.7 | .. | .. | 47 |
| Iceland | ◆ | 0.4 | .. | .. | 89 | .. | .. |
| Italy | ◆ | 0.5 | 0.3 | 0.9 | 84 | 51 | 135 |
| Netherlands | ◆ | 1.2 | 0.7 | 1.9 | 206 | 130 | 336 |
| Norway | ◆ | .. | .. | 1.2 | .. | .. | 210 |
| Poland | ◆ | 0.3 | 0.8 | 1.1 | 19 | 42 | 61 |
| Portugal | ◆ | 0.6 | 0.1 | 0.7 | 70 | 16 | 87 |
| Spain | ◆ | 0.5 | 0.3 | 0.8 | 65 | 40 | 105 |
| Sweden | ◆ | 0.8 | 0.3 | 1.2 | 139 | 55 | 194 |
| Switzerland | ◆ | 1.0 | 0.6 | 1.6 | 240 | 135 | 376 |
| United Kingdom | ◆ | 0.4 | 0.6 | 1.0 | 65 | 92 | 157 |

*excluding households.

◆ See Technical Annex for data sources, notes and comments.

**STATE AND TRENDS
SUMMARY**

PAC expenditure is part of environmental protection expenditure, covering curative and preventive measures measures directly aimed at pollution abatement and control. PAC expenditure as a percentage of GDP is slowly growing as stronger pollution prevention and control polices are implemented. It now generally amounts to 1 to 2 per cent of GDP in most OECD countries. In general, the investment-related share of PAC decreases as investment programmes progress, while operating expenses' share grows. In countries with small GDP, a low level of expenditure in GDP terms means PAC is very limited.

Public sector PAC measures mainly concern sewerage, waste water treatment and the collection and disposal of municipal waste. Such measures generally represent 0.4 to 0.9 per cent of GDP. Public expenditure on water is usually large, and growing in line with efforts to ensure that most of the population is connected to sewerage and public waste water treatment. Public expenditure is generally financed by pollution taxes or charges paid by households, but most countries still fund PAC partly from the general budget.

Private sector (business) measures mostly relate to air and water pollution and hazardous waste disposal. They generally amount to 0.5 to 0.9 per cent of GDP. They mainly represent compliance with the polluter pays principle. Business also pays pollution charges to public authorities, either to offset costs of services or in relation to externalities.

## OFFICIAL DEVELOPMENT ASSISTANCE 33

### Trends in Official Development Assistance, 1980-96
### as % of GNP

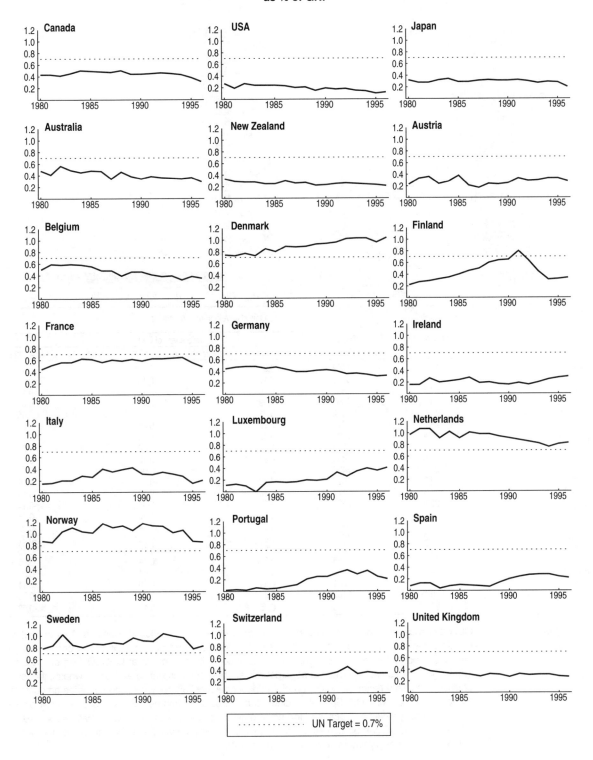

············· UN Target = 0.7%

*OECD Environmental Indicators  1998*

## OFFICIAL DEVELOPMENT ASSISTANCE 33

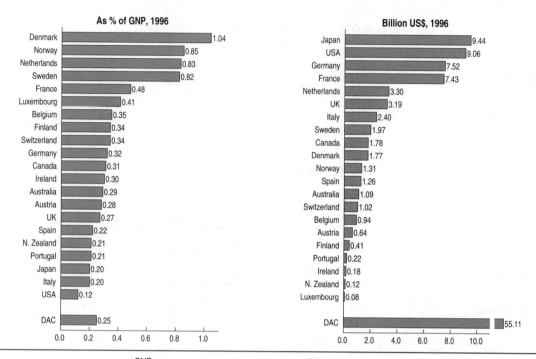

| | GNP per capita 1 000 US$/cap. | Official development assistance Total, 1996 million US$ | as a share of GNP %, 1996 | as a share of GNP absolute change since 1980 | as a share of GNP absolute change since 1992 |
|---|---|---|---|---|---|
| Canada | 19.2 | 1782 | 0.31 | -0.12 | -0.15 |
| USA | 28.4 | 9058 | 0.12 | -0.15 | -0.06 |
| Japan | 37.5 | 9437 | 0.20 | -0.12 | -0.10 |
| Australia | 20.6 | 1093 | 0.29 | -0.19 | -0.07 |
| New Zealand | 16.0 | 122 | 0.21 | -0.12 | -0.05 |
| Austria | 28.2 | 640 | 0.28 | 0.05 | -0.01 |
| Belgium | 26.4 | 937 | 0.35 | -0.15 | -0.03 |
| Denmark | 32.4 | 1773 | 1.04 | 0.30 | 0.02 |
| Finland | 23.5 | 409 | 0.34 | 0.12 | -0.30 |
| France | 26.5 | 7430 | 0.48 | 0.04 | -0.14 |
| Germany | 28.7 | 7515 | 0.32 | -0.12 | -0.03 |
| Ireland | 16.3 | 177 | 0.30 | 0.14 | 0.14 |
| Italy | 20.9 | 2397 | 0.20 | 0.05 | -0.14 |
| Luxembourg | 44.9 | 77 | 0.41 | 0.30 | 0.15 |
| Netherlands | 25.7 | 3303 | 0.83 | -0.14 | -0.02 |
| Norway | 35.3 | 1311 | 0.85 | -0.02 | -0.27 |
| Portugal | 10.6 | 221 | 0.21 | 0.19 | -0.15 |
| Spain | 14.6 | 1258 | 0.22 | 0.14 | -0.05 |
| Sweden | 27.0 | 1968 | 0.82 | 0.04 | -0.21 |
| Switzerland | 42.4 | 1021 | 0.34 | 0.10 | -0.11 |
| UK | 20.1 | 3185 | 0.27 | -0.08 | -0.03 |
| DAC | 27.0 | 55114 | 0.25 | -0.10 | -0.08 |

**STATE AND TRENDS SUMMARY**

ODA is provided to support socio-economic development of less developed countries. A large fraction of ODA aims at ensuring more sustainable development and, in particular, conserving natural resources and protecting the environment. Despite commitments made at UNCED (Rio de Janeiro, 1992), ODA is decreasing. There is no direct relation between assistance and donor wealth; the level of discrepancy is a factor of more than eight. Most countries' aid to developing countries amounts to 0.2 to 0.4 per cent of GDP. Special funding via the Global Environment Facility is directed at global environmental problems. Total aid for environmental protection is relatively small. About 10 to 25 per cent of ODA can be related to drinking water provision, river management, soil conservation, tropical forest management, nature protection and PAC.

# IV. OECD FRAMEWORK FOR ENVIRONMENTAL INDICATORS

# OECD FRAMEWORK FOR ENVIRONMENTAL INDICATORS

The OECD environmental indicators programme recognises that there is no universal set of indicators; rather, several sets exist, corresponding to specific purposes. Indicators can be used at international and national levels in state of the environment reporting, measurement of environmental performance and reporting on progress towards sustainable development. They can further be used at national level in planning, clarifying policy objectives and setting priorities.

The OECD work focuses principally on indicators to be used in national, international and global decision making, yet the approach may also be used to develop indicators at subnational or ecosystem level.

## SEVERAL TYPES OF INDICATORS

The OECD work[1] includes several types of environmental indicators, each corresponding to a specific purpose and framework:

♦ the OECD Core Set of environmental indicators, to keep track of environmental progress;

♦ several sets of sectoral indicators, to promote integration of environmental concerns into sectoral policy making: transport-environment indicators, energy-environment indicators, agri-environmental indicators[2];

♦ indicators derived from environmental accounting, to promote both integration of environmental concerns into economic policies and sustainable use and management of natural resources.

All these indicator sets are closely related to each other, the OECD Core Set being a synthesis and representing a common minimum set; i.e. the most important sectoral indicators are part of the Core Set, as are major indicators derived from resource accounting.

## APPROACH AND RESULTS

In developing harmonised international environmental indicators, OECD countries adopted a pragmatic approach, which led in particular to:

♦ agreement on a common conceptual framework, based on a common understanding of concepts and definitions and on the pressure-state-response (PSR) model (Inset 1, Inset 3);

♦ identification of criteria to help in selecting indicators and validating their choice: all indicators are reviewed according to their policy relevance, analytical soundness and measurability (Inset 2);

♦ identification and definition of indicators (including an assessment of their measurability);

♦ provision of guidance for the use of indicators (stressing that indicators are only one tool and have to be interpreted in context).

Those indicators for which internationally comparable data exist are regularly published and used in current OECD work, particularly in OECD environmental performance reviews.

Building on experience in environmental information and reporting and on strong support from Member countries, results of this work, and in particular its conceptual framework, have in turn influenced similar activities by a number of countries and international organisations.

---

1. *Like other work on environmental information and reporting, the work on environmental indicators is led by the OECD Group on the State of the Environment.*
2. *Work led by the Joint Working Party of the Agriculture Committee and the Environmental Policy Committee.*

---

## Inset 1  Definitions and functions of environmental indicators

The terminology adopted by OECD countries points to two major functions of indicators:

♦ they reduce the number of measurements and parameters that normally would be required to give an "exact" presentation of a situation;

♦ they simplify the communication process by which the results of measurement are provided to the user.

### TERMINOLOGY

♦ Indicator: A parameter, or a value derived from parameters, which points to, provides information about, describes the state of a phenomenon/environment/area, with a significance extending beyond that directly associated with a parameter value.

♦ Index: A set of aggregated or weighted parameters or indicators.

♦ Parameter: A property that is measured or observed.

---

## Inset 2  Criteria for selecting environmental indicators

As indicators are used for various purposes, it is necessary to define general criteria for selecting indicators. Three basic criteria are used in OECD work: policy relevance and utility for users, analytical soundness, and measurability.*

**POLICY RELEVANCE**     An environmental indicator should:

♦ provide a representative picture of environmental conditions, pressures on the environment or society's responses;
♦ be simple, easy to interpret and able to show trends over time;
♦ be responsive to changes in the environment and related human activities;
♦ provide a basis for international comparisons;
♦ be either national in scope or applicable to regional environmental issues of national significance;
♦ have a threshold or reference value against which to compare it, so that users can assess the significance of the values associated with it.

**ANALYTICAL SOUNDNESS**     An environmental indicator should:

♦ be theoretically well founded in technical and scientific terms;
♦ be based on international standards and international consensus about its validity;
♦ lend itself to being linked to economic models, forecasting and information systems.

**MEASURABILITY**     The data required to support the indicator should be:

♦ readily available or made available at a reasonable cost/benefit ratio;
♦ adequately documented and of known quality;
♦ updated at regular intervals in accordance with reliable procedures.

---

*\* These criteria describe the "ideal" indicator; not all of them will be met in practice.*

### Inset 3 **The Pressure - State - Response (PSR) Model**

The PSR model considers that: human activities exert <u>pressures</u> on the environment and affect its quality and the quantity of natural resources ("<u>state</u>"); society responds to these changes through environmental, general economic and sectoral policies and through changes in awareness and behaviour ("<u>societal response</u>"). The PSR model has the advantage of highlighting these links, and helping decision makers and the public see environmental and other issues as interconnected (although this should not obscure the view of more complex relationships in ecosystems, and in environment-economy and environment-social interactions).

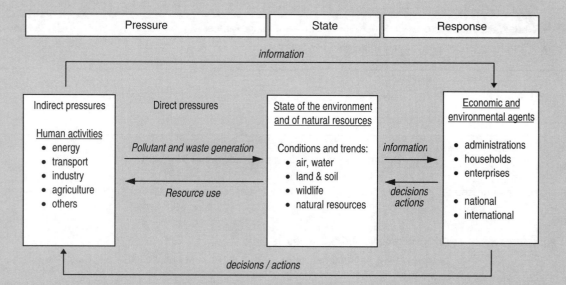

Depending on the purpose for which the PSR model is to be used, it can easily be adjusted to account for greater details or for specific features. Examples of adjusted versions are the Driving force - State - Reponse (DSR) model used by the UNCSD in its work on sustainable development indicators, the framework used for OECD sectoral indicators (see page 111) and the Driving force - Pressure - State - Impact - Response (DPSIR) model used by the European Environment Agency.

# THE OECD CORE SET OF ENVIRONMENTAL INDICATORS

## PURPOSE AND CHARACTERISTICS

The OECD Core Set of environmental indicators is a commonly agreed upon set of indicators for OECD countries and for international use, published regularly. It is a first step in tracking environmental progress and the factors involved in it, and it is a major tool for measuring environmental performance. Characteristics of the Core Set are that:

- it is of limited size (around 50 indicators);
- it covers a broad range of environmental issues;
- it reflects an approach common to a majority of OECD countries.

## FRAMEWORK

### THE PSR MODEL

Firstly, the PSR model provides a classification into indicators of environmental pressures, indicators of environmental conditions and indicators of societal responses:

♦ Indicators of environmental pressures describe pressures from human activities exerted on the environment, including natural resources. "Pressures" here cover underlying or indirect pressures (i.e. the activity itself and trends of environmental significance) as well as proximate or direct pressures (i.e. the use of resources and the discharge of pollutants and waste materials). Indicators of environmental pressures are closely related to production and consumption patterns; they often reflect emission or resource use intensities, along with related trends and changes over a given period. They can be used to show progress in decoupling economic activities from related environmental pressures. They can also be used to show progress in meeting national objectives and international commitments (e.g. emission reduction targets).

♦ Indicators of environmental conditions relate to the quality of the environment and the quality and quantity of natural resources. As such they reflect the ultimate objective of environmental policies. Indicators of environmental conditions are designed to give an overview of the situation (the state) concerning the environment and its development over time. Examples of indicators of environmental conditions are: concentration of pollutants in environmental media, exceedance of critical loads, population exposure to certain levels of pollution or degrated environmental quality, the status of wildlife and of natural resource stocks. In practice, measuring environmental conditions can be difficult or very costly. Therefore, environmental pressures are often measured instead as a substitute.

♦ Indicators of societal responses show the extent to which society responds to environmental concerns. They refer to individual and collective actions and reactions, intended to:

- mitigate, adapt to or prevent human-induced negative effects on the environment;
- halt or reverse environmental damage already inflicted;
- preserve and conserve nature and natural resources.

Examples of indicators of societal responses are environmental expenditure, environment-related taxes and subsidies, price structures, market shares of environmentally friendly goods and services, pollution abatement rates, waste recycling rates. In practice, indicators mostly relate to abatement and control measures; those showing preventive and integrative measures and actions are more difficult to obtain.

### MAJOR ISSUES OF CONCERN

Secondly, the second dimension of the Core Set structure distinguishes a number of environmental issues that reflect major environmental concerns in OECD countries. For each issue, indicators of environmental pressure, conditions and societal responses have been defined (Inset 4).

Inset 4 **Structure of OECD Indicators Core Set by Environmental Issue**

| Major issues | PRESSURE Indicators of environmental pressures | STATE Indicators of environmental conditions | RESPONSE Indicators of societal responses |
|---|---|---|---|
| 1. Climate change | | | |
| 2. Ozone layer depletion | | | |
| 3. Eutrophication | | | |
| 4. Acidification | | | |
| 5. Toxic contamination | | | |
| 6. Urban environmental quality | | | |
| 7. Biodiversity | | | |
| 8. Cultural landscapes | | | |
| 9. Waste | | | |
| 10. Water resources | | | |
| 11. Forest resources | | | |
| 12. Fish resources | | | |
| 13. Soil degradation (desertification, erosion) | | | |
| 14. Socio-economic, sectoral and background indicators | | | |

Broadly speaking, the first nine issues relate to the use of the environment's "sink capacity", dealing with issues of environmental quality, whereas the other issues relate to the environment's "source capacity", focusing on the quantity aspect of natural resources.

Not all indicators can be directly associated with a specific environmental issue. Some reflect background variables and driving forces, such as population growth and economic growth; others deal with selected sectoral trends and patterns of environmental significance, or factors such as economy-wide environmental expenditure and public opinion. An additional category of indicators has therefore been introduced in the framework. This category also provides an opportunity to further integrate indicators from sectoral sets into the OECD Core Set.

These issues depend on changing and sometimes conflicting perceptions; the list is not necessarily final or exhaustive.

**SECTORAL BREAKDOWN**

Thirdly and in the longer term, the possibility of disaggregating major indicators at <u>sectoral level</u> is considered. Data availability permitting, this is one tool for analysing environmental pressures exerted by different economic sectors and distinguishing government responses from those of the business sector or private households. Indicators at the sectoral level could be useful in reviewing the integration of environmental and sectoral policies and monitoring resource use and emission intensities in the various economic sectors. Indicators at sectoral level also facilitate the link with economic information systems and models.

# THE OECD SETS OF SECTORAL INDICATORS

## PURPOSE AND CHARACTERISTICS

The OECD has been developing sets of sectoral indicators to <u>better integrate environmental concerns into sectoral policies</u>. The objective is to develop a "tool kit" for sectoral decision makers, which should facilitate the integration of environmental concerns in sectoral policy making. While limited to a specific sector and its interactions with the environment, these indicators are typically developed in larger numbers than the Core Set.

Sectoral indicator sets are not restricted to "environmental indicators" *per se* but also concern linkages between the environment and the economy, placed in a context of sustainable development. They may include environmental indicators (e.g. pollutant emissions), economic indicators (e.g. sectoral output, prices and taxes, subisidies) and selected social indicators.

## FRAMEWORK

The <u>conceptual framework adopted for sectoral indicators</u> (Inset 5) is derived from the PSR model, but was adjusted to account for the specificities of the respective sectors. As defined by OECD countries, sectoral indicators have been organised along a framework that distinguishes:

♦ indicators to reflect sectoral trends and patterns of environmental significance (i.e. indirect pressures and/or related driving forces);

♦ indicators to reflect interactions between the sector and the environment, including positive and negative effects of sectoral activity on the environment (i.e. direct pressures, such as pollutant releases and resource use, and related effects and resulting environmental conditions, such as ambient concentrations of pollutants and population exposure), as well as effects of environmental changes on sectoral activity;

♦ indicators to reflect economic linkages between the sector and the environment, as well as policy considerations. This category includes environmental damage and environmental expenditure, economic and fiscal instruments, and trade issues.

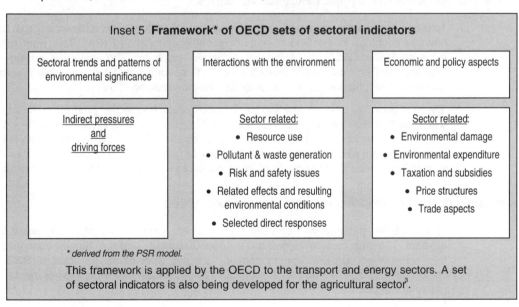

**Inset 5  Framework\* of OECD sets of sectoral indicators**

| Sectoral trends and patterns of environmental significance | Interactions with the environment | Economic and policy aspects |
|---|---|---|
| <u>Indirect pressures</u><br><u>and</u><br><u>driving forces</u> | <u>Sector related:</u><br>• Resource use<br>• Pollutant & waste generation<br>• Risk and safety issues<br>• Related effects and resulting environmental conditions<br>• Selected direct responses | <u>Sector related:</u><br>• Environmental damage<br>• Environmental expenditure<br>• Taxation and subsidies<br>• Price structures<br>• Trade aspects |

*\* derived from the PSR model.*

This framework is applied by the OECD to the transport and energy sectors. A set of sectoral indicators is also being developed for the agricultural sector[3].

---

3.  📖 *OECD (1993), Indicators for the Integration of Environmental Concerns into Transport Policies*
    📖 *OECD (1993), Indicators for the Integration of Environmental Concerns into Energy Policies*
    📖 *OECD (1997), Environmental Indicators for Agriculture*

# OECD ENVIRONMENTAL ACCOUNTING

Environmental indicators are also derived from the broader area of environmental accounting, in both physical and monetary terms[4]. The OECD work focuses on physical natural resource accounts as a tool for sustainable management of natural resources, as well as on expenditure for pollution abatement and control and other environmental measures. In addition, the OECD participates in international work on environmental accounting and acts as a forum for exchanges of experiences in this field. (Inset 6)

---

### Inset 6  Environmental accounting: definitions and concepts

Environmental accounting can be defined as the systematic description of interactions between the environment and the economy by means of an accounting framework. There is no unique model for environmental accounting; approaches vary according to purpose.

| Approach | Environmental categories taken into account | Characteristics |
|---|---|---|
| Adjustment of national economic accounts | Valuation of:<br>♦ Environmental damages<br>♦ Environmental services<br>♦ Stock of natural capital | Modifies SNA framework and boundaries |
| Satellite accounts | Valuation of:<br>♦ Environmental damages<br>♦ Environmental services<br>♦ Stock of natural capital<br>♦ Environmental expenditure<br>Corresponding physical flows and stocks | Complements SNA without modifying it General coherence with SNA |
| Natural resource and environment accounts | ♦ Physical flows and stocks of natural resources<br>♦ Physical and monetary flows associated with anthropogenic exploitation of natural resources | Independent from and complementary to SNA |

---

## INDICATORS DERIVED FROM NATURAL RESOURCE ACCOUNTS

To progress towards a common methodology, the OECD reviewed different approaches of OECD Member countries in the field of natural resource accounting (NRA). This work resulted in the establishment of OECD pilot accounts on forests and water. The basic methodology used in the pilot accounts is simple and provides a guide to countries that are developing natural resource accounts. The format was set up to provide a tool for decision makers.

The pilot accounts propose physical input-output tables tracing the production, transformation and use of each resource throughout the economy. This provides an analytical tool with which to assess the impact of sectoral economic activity on the resource. Basic flow relations from these accounts form the input for calculating indicators of sustainable use of natural resource quantities. Examples of such indicators are: intensity of use of forest resources and intensity of use of water resources.

## INDICATORS DERIVED FROM ENVIRONMENTAL EXPENDITURE ACCOUNTS

The OECD has pursued work on pollution abatement and control (PAC) expenditure for a number of years. The data thus developed are published regularly and supplement economic information from national accounts. Indicators derived from this work reflect the level of PAC expenditure compared with GDP, as well as the structure of such expenditure per environmental domain and per source sector.

---

4.  OECD (1996), *Environmental Accounting for Decision Making - Summary Report of an OECD Seminar*
     OECD (1996), *Natural Resource Accounts - Taking Stock in OECD Countries*
     OECD (1996), *Pollution Abatement and Control Expenditure in OECD Countries*

# USING ENVIRONMENTAL INDICATORS

## GUIDING PRINCIPLES

When using environmental indicators in analytical and evaluation work, the OECD applies the following principles:

### ONLY ONE TOOL

Indicators are only one tool for evaluation; scientific and policy-oriented interpretation is required for them to acquire their full meaning. They often need to be supplemented by other qualitative and scientific information, particularly in explaining driving forces behind indicator changes which form the basis for an assessment.

### THE APPROPRIATE CONTEXT

Indicators' relevance varies by country and by context. They must be reported and interpreted in the appropriate context, taking into account countries' different ecological, geographical, social, economic and institutional features.

In the OECD environmental performance reviews, international indicators derived from the Core Set are generally used in combination with specific national indicators and data. These national indicators provide a more detailed picture of the country's situation through further sectoral and/or spatial breakdown (e.g. subnational data) and often point at particular issues of concern.

### INTERCOUNTRY COMPARISON AND STANDARDISATION

OECD focuses on national indicators for use in international work. This implies not only nationally aggregated indicators, but also an appropriate level of comparability among countries. Despite a number of achievements in this area, further work is needed on internationally harmonised definitions and concepts.

There is no single method of standardisation for the comparison of environmental indicators across countries. The outcome of the assessment may depend on the chosen denominator (e.g. GDP, population, land area) as well as on national definitions and measurement methods. It is therefore appropriate for different denominators to be used in parallel to balance the message conveyed. In some cases absolute values may be the appropriate measure, for example when international commitments are linked to absolute values.

## MEASURABILITY

Measurability issues such as the quality of underlying data are important in the use of environmental indicators, and must be taken into account to avoid misinterpretation.

Measurability still varies greatly among individual indicators. Some indicators are immediately measurable, others need additional efforts before they can be published. For example, most indicators of societal responses have a shorter history than indicators of environmental pressures and many indicators of environmental conditions, and are still in development both conceptually and in terms of data availability.

### TIMELINESS

Another important criterion affecting the usefulness and relevance of an indicator is the timeliness of the underlying data. The interval between the period to which data refer and the date when data are released should be as short as is practicable. Current timeliness of environmental data remains insufficient and needs improvement as a matter of priority.

## LEVEL OF AGGREGATION

Most OECD indicators focus on the national level and are designed to be used in an international context. Within a country a greater level of detail or breakdown may be needed, particularly when indicators are to support subnational or sectoral decision making or when national indicators hide major regional differences. This is particularly important when dealing, for example, with river basin or ecosystem management. The actual measurement of indicators at these levels is encouraged and lies within the responsibility of individual countries. At these levels, however, measurability and comparability problems may be further exacerbated.

## ENVIRONMENTAL INDICATORS AND PERFORMANCE ANALYSIS

In the OECD context, environmental indicators are used as a tool for evaluating environmental performance. They support the analysis made in OECD country environmental performance reviews[5] and provide all reviews with a common denominator. This creates a synergy in which regular feedback is provided on the indicators' policy relevance and analytical soundness.

Using environmental indicators in environmental performance reviews implies linking these indicators to the measurement and analysis of achievements, as well as to underlying driving forces and to the country's specific conditions. Indicators can be linked to:

♦ explicit quantitative objectives (goals, targets, commitments);

♦ broad qualitative objectives concerning, for example:
   - efficiency of human activities (linked to the notions of decoupling, elasticities, integration);
   - sustainability of natural resource use and development.

It is important to recognise, however, that indicators are not a mechanical measure of environmental performance. They need to be complemented with background information, analysis and interpretation.

---

5. The <u>OECD Environmental Performance Review Programme</u>, assesses Member countries' performance by comparing achievements or progress with national objectives and international commitments. The reviews take into account each country's absolute levels of environmental quality and the physical, human and economic context.

&#x1F4D6; OECD, Environmental Performance Reviews. 4 reviews published each year. Already published: Austria, Belarus, Bulgaria, Canada, Finland, France, Germany, Iceland, Italy, Japan, Korea, Netherlands, New Zealand, Norway, Poland, Portugal, Spain, Sweden, United Kingdom, United States.

# V.    TECHNICAL ANNEX

# GENERAL INFORMATION

**Country region codes used are as follows:**

| | | | | | |
|---|---|---|---|---|---|
| CAN: | Canada | FIN: | Finland | NOR: | Norway |
| MEX: | Mexico | FRA: | France | POL: | Poland |
| USA: | United States | DEU: | Germany | PRT: | Portugal |
| JPN: | Japan | wDEU: | western Germany | ESP: | Spain |
| KOR: | Korea | GRC: | Greece | SWE: | Sweden |
| AUS: | Australia | HUN: | Hungary | CHE: | Switzerland |
| NZL: | New Zealand | ISL: | Iceland | TUR: | Turkey |
| AUT: | Austria | IRL: | Ireland | UKD: | United Kingdom |
| BEL: | Belgium | ITA: | Italy | TOT: | regional totals |
| CZE: | Czech Republic | LUX: | Luxembourg | DAC: | OECD Development Assistance |
| DNK: | Denmark | NLD: | Netherlands | | Committee Member countries |

*: Data including western Germany only

➤ **Country aggregates**

OECD: All OECD Member countries, which include the OECD Europe — i.e. countries of the European Union (EU) plus Czech Republic, Hungary, Iceland, Norway, Poland, Switzerland and Turkey — plus Canada, Mexico, the United States, Japan, Korea, Australia and New Zealand.

OECD* All OECD Member countries except eastern Germany.

OECD** Partial OECD total.

➤ **Signs**

| | | | | | |
|---|---|---|---|---|---|
| ..; n.a. | not available | . | decimal point | % | percentage |
| - | nil or negligible | n. app. | not applicable | $ | US dollar |

➤ **Abbreviations**

| | | | | | |
|---|---|---|---|---|---|
| BOD | - biochemical oxygen demand | HCFC | - hydrochlorofluorocarbon | ODA | - official development assistance |
| Cap | - capita | HM | - heavy metal | PAC | - pollution abatement & control |
| CFC | - chlorofluorocarbon | Inh | - inhabitant | PCB | - polychlorinated biphenyls |
| CO | - carbon monoxide | kcal | - kilocalorie | PFC | - private final consumption |
| $CO_2$ | - carbon dioxide | L | - litre | Pop | - population |
| $CH_4$ | - methane | Mtoe | - million tonnes of oil equivalent | ppb | - parts per billion |
| DAC | - Development Assistance Committee. | N | - nitrogen | PPP | - purchasing power parities |
| | | $N_2O$ | - nitrous oxide | ppt | - parts per trillion |
| GCV | - gross calorific value | $NO_x$ | - nitrogen oxides | $SO_x$ | - sulphur oxides |
| GDP | - gross domestic product | NMVOC | - non-methane volatile organic compounds | t | - tonne |
| GNP | - gross national product | | | veh-km | - vehicle-kilometre |
| GHG | - greenhouse gas | | | | |

➤ **Units**

| | | | | | |
|---|---|---|---|---|---|
| cal | - calorie (1 cal = 4.1868 joules) | kWh | - kilowatt hour (1 kWh = 103 Wh = 0.8598 kilocalories) | $m^3$ | - cubic metre (1 $m^3$ = 1.3079 cubic yards) |
| Dobson | - see Ozone Layer Depletion notes | | | | |
| g | - gram (1 g = 0.0353 ounces) | | | Toe | - tonne of oil equivalent |
| $\mu g$ | - microgram (1 $\mu g$ = $10^{-6}$ g) | litre | - (1 l = 1 $dm^3$ = 0.001 $m^3$) | | (1 Toe = $10^7$ kcal = 41.868*$10^9$ joules) |
| mg | - milligram (1 mg = $10^{-3}$ g) | km | - kilometre | tonne | - metric ton |
| ha | - hectare (1 ha = 0.01 $km^2$) | | (1 km = 1 000 m. = 0.6214 miles) | | (1 t. = 1 000 kg = 0.9842 long ton |
| kg | - kilogram (1 kg = 1 000 g = 2.2046 pounds) | $km^2$ | - square kilometre (1 $km^2$ = 0.3861 square miles) | | = 1.1023 short ton) |

➤ **Per capita values**

All <u>per capita</u> information uses OECD and Food and Agriculture Organization (FAO) population data.

➤ **Per unit of GDP values**

All <u>per unit of GDP</u> information uses OECD GDP data at 1991 prices and purchasing power parties (PPPs). The use of PPPs appears preferable to the use of exchange rates in conjunction with environmental questions, as the objective of comparing measures of economic activity such as GDP is to reflect underlying volumes and physical processes as closely as possible.

PPPs are defined as the ratio between the amount of national currency and the amount of a reference currency needed to buy the same bundle of consumption goods in the two countries. In this publication, the reference currency is US$. Typically, PPPs differ from exchange rates as the latter reflect not only relative prices of consumer goods but also a host of other factors, including international capital movements, interest rate differentials and government intervention. As a consequence, exchange rates exhibit much greater variations over time than PPPs.

# CLIMATE CHANGE

♦ A number of gases have <u>direct effects</u> on climate change and are considered responsible for a major part of global warming: carbon dioxide ($CO_2$), methane ($CH_4$), nitrous oxide ($N_2O$), chlorofluorocarbons (CFCs), hydrofluorocarbons (HCFCs), methyl bromide ($CH_3Br$) and sulphur hexa fluoride ($SF_6$). Other air pollutants, such as NMVOC, $NO_x$ and CO, have <u>indirect effects</u> on climate change as their reactions in the atmosphere result in the production of tropospheric ozone which effectively a GHG. Sulphur-containing trace gases also play a role. A major part of these emissions stems from combustion of fossil fuels and biomass. Other sources are industrial processes, agriculture and changes in land use.

## CO2 EMISSION INTENSITIES

Data sources:   IEA-OECD

♦ Data refer to <u>gross direct emissions</u>; $CO_2$ removal by sinks, indirect emissions from land use changes and indirect effects through interactions in the atmosphere are not taken into account.

♦ Data refer to $CO_2$ emissions from <u>fossil fuel combustion</u>. Anthropogenic emissions by other sources (industrial processes, biomass burning) are not included.

♦ Data are estimates based on the default methods and emission factors from the *Revised 1996 IPCC Guidelines for National Greenhouse Gas Inventories* and on the IEA-OECD data for total primary energy supply.

## GREENHOUSE GAS CONCENTRATIONS

Data sources:    World Resources Institute (WRI), *World Resources 1996-1997, A guide to the global environment* based on data from CDIAC (Carbon Dioxide Information Analysis Center).

♦ Although gas concentrations at any given time vary among monitoring sites, the data reported reflect global trends. $CO_2$ data refer to Mauna Loa, Hawaii (19°32′ N, 155°35′ W). Data for other gases are from values monitored at Cape Grim, Tasmania (45°41′

♦ Oil and gas for non-energy purposes such as feedstocks in the chemical and petrochemical industries are excluded.

♦ Oil held in international marine bunkers is excluded at national level; world emissions include marine bunkers, amounting to 410 million tonnes in 1995.

♦ Further details on calculation methods and conversion factors can be found in *IEA-OECD (1997), CO2 Emissions from Fuel Combustion , A new basis for comparing emis. of a major greenhouse gas , 1972-95.*

♦ For details on fuel supply and energy prices see Energy notes.

♦ Energy prices: % change refer to 1980-95 period.

MEX  ➢ Energy prices: % change refer to 1982-95 period.

S, 144°41′ E) under the Atmospheric Lifetime Experiment (ALE) and Global Atmospheric Gases Experiment (GAGE).

♦ Total gaseous chlorine concentrations: calculated by multiplying the number of chlorine atoms in each of the chlorine-containing gases (carbon tetrachloride ($CCl_4$), methyl chloroform ($CH_3CCl_3$), CFC-11 ($CCl_3F$), CFC-12 ($CCl_2F_2$), CFC-22 ($CHClF_2$), and CFC-113 ($C_2Cl_3F_3$)) by the concentration of that gas.

♦ For further details, please refer to the above-cited WRI publication.

# OZONE LAYER DEPLETION

## OZONE DEPLETING SUBSTANCES

Data sources      Ozone Secretariat/UNEP Nairobi;  OECD

♦ <u>CFCs:</u> Annex A Group I substances (chlorofluorocarbons).
♦ <u>Halons:</u> Annex A Group II substances (halons).
♦ <u>Other CFCs:</u> Annex B Group I, II and III substances (other fully halogenated CFCs, carbon tetrachloride and methyl chloroform).
♦ <u>HCFCs:</u> Annex C Group I substances (hydrochlorofluorocarbons).
♦ <u>Methyl bromide:</u> Annex E.

## STRATOSPHERIC OZONE

Data sources:    Column ozone: WODC (World Ozone Data Center). Global ozone levels: Ozone Processing Team of NASA/Goddard Space Flight Center.

♦ Data refer to <u>total column ozone</u> (i.e. tropospheric plus stratospheric ozone) in Dobson units. Stratospheric ozone represents the majority of total column ozone, e.g. stratospheric ozone, on average, comprises about 90% of total column ozone in Canada. A <u>Dobson unit</u> is a measure used to estimate the thickness of the ozone layer. 100 Dobson units represent a quantity equivalent to a 1-mm-thick layer of ozone at 0 degrees Celsius and at a pressure of 1013 hectopascal (sea level).

♦ Data are weighted with the ozone depleting potentials of the substances.
♦ Regional totals include OECD Secretariat estimates.
♦ Dotted lines (graphics) refer to data not available.
NAM  ➢ Excludes Mexico (Article 5 country).
OECD ➢ Excludes Mexico, Rep. Korea and Turkey (Article 5 countries).

♦ Ozone levels over selected cities: data presented are annual averages of daily values taken from the WODC database calculated by the OECD Secretariat.

♦ Global ozone levels: data are annual averages generated from daily ozone measurements. Ozone was measured by the Total Ozone Mapping Spectrometer (TOMS) on the Nimbus-7 (1979-1992), and the Meteor-3 (1992-1993) satellites, referring to latitudes between 70 ° N and 70 ° S. At latitudes above 70 °, ozone data are not collected during the winter months and there is increasing seasonal and interannual variability.

# AIR QUALITY

## SOx AND NOx EMISSIONS

Data sources:    OECD, UN/ECE

♦ Data refer to man-made emissions only. $SO_x$ and $NO_x$ data are given as quantities of $SO_2$ and $NO_2$ respectively.

♦ Emissions from international transport (aviation and marine) are excluded.

♦ Data may include provisional figures and Secretariat estimates.

♦ % change: refers to change with respect to the latest available year from 1990 on.

♦ For further details, please refer to *OECD Environmental Data — Compendium 1997.*

♦ National targets: current reduction targets as submitted by the Parties to the Convention on Long-Range Transboundary Air Pollution.

CAN  ➢ $SO_x$: $SO_2$ only.

USA ➤ SOx: SO2 only.

JPN ➤ SOx and NOx mid 1990s: 1992 data including Secretariat estimates for road transport emissions based on road transport fuel consumption data. NOx % change since 1987: based on estimated data for 1987.

KOR ➤ SOx: SO2 only, excluding industrial processes. NOx: NO2 only. Break in time series in 1990 due to a change in the emission coefficient of industrial fuel combustion.

AUS ➤ NOx data source: Australia's National GHG Inventory. More than one-third of NOx come from control burning savannahs.

AUT ➤ SOx: SO2 only. Break in time series in 1992 and 1994. NOx: break in time series in 1992; national objectives refer to the 1992 Ozone Act and to the years 1996, 2001 and 2006.

CZE ➤ SOx: SO2 only.

DNK ➤ Inventory data based on diesel and gasoline sales in Denmark. Mid 1990s: estimates based on CORINAIR method.

FRA ➤ NOx: change in estimation methodology in 1990.

DEU ➤ SOx: change in estimation methodology in 1991.

GRC ➤ Mid 1990s: 1990 data.

HUN ➤ SOx: SO2 only.

ISL ➤ % change refers to the period 1982-95. SOx: SO2 only.

IRL ➤ Emissions from industrial processes are excluded.

ITA ➤ Pre 1985 data exclude industrial processes. Mid 1990s: 1992 data.

LUX ➤ NOx: % change since 1987: based on estimated data for 1987.

NLD ➤ Estimation methodology changed in 1992.

PRT ➤ SOx: Break in time series in 1990. Pre-1990 data refer to SO2 only. NOx: % change since 1987: based on estimated data for 1987; national data may differ.

ESP ➤ 1980: Secretariat estimate. Break in time series in 1985 and 1990 (CORINAIR 85 and 90). NOx: % change since 1987: based on estimated data for 1987.

SWE ➤ NOx: % change since 1987: based on estimated data for 1987.

UKD ➤ SOx: SO2 only.

OECD ➤ Secretariat estimates.

## URBAN AIR QUALITY (SO2 AND NO2)

Data sources:  OECD

CAN ➤ Measurement temperature: - 15.6°C.

JPN ➤ Fiscal year. Measurement temperature 20°C.

FIN ➤ Measurement temperature 20°C. NO2: data refer to traffic sites near city centre.

FRA ➤ 1994 data are provisional. Paris (SO2): Paris agglomeration.

ISL ➤ SO2: 1990 data refer to mean concentrations for the months 09 to 12. NO2: measuring station located near a busy street corner and unusually close to traffic in 1995.

LUX ➤ NO2: data refer to city centre.

NOR ➤ SO2: fiscal year; data refer to the mean pollution level of St Olavsplass and Bryn skole. NO2: monitoring period from Oct. to March; data refer to St. Olavsplass/Nardahl Bruns St.

PRT ➤ SO2: in 1992 six UV Fluor. stations were incorporated.

ESP ➤ The number of monitoring stations differs from year to year. Madrid: data refer to city centre.

SWE ➤ Monitoring period from October to March. Stockholm: the number of monitoring stations changed during the series.

TUR ➤ NO2: base reference refers to 1993.

UKD ➤ Fiscal year. Measurement method follows British Standard 1747 Part. 3.

### SO2

| | Cat. (a) | City or area | Measurement method | No. Stn. (b) |
|---|---|---|---|---|
| Canada | A | Montreal | UV Fluor. | 7 |
| | B | Hamilton | UV Fluor. | 3 |
| Mexico | B | Mexico City | .. | 5 |
| USA | A | New York | .. | 13 |
| | A | Los Angeles | .. | 6 |
| Japan | A | Tokyo | Conduct. c. | 20-16 |
| | B | Kawasaki | Conduct. c. | 7-8 |
| Korea | A | Seoul | UV Fluor. | 20 |
| | A | Pusan | UV Fluor. | 7 |
| Austria | A | Wien | .. | 14 |
| | B | Linz | .. | 7 |
| Belgium | A | Bruxelles | UV Fluor. | 8-6 |
| | B | Antwerpen | UV Fluor. | 12-8 |
| Czech. R. | A | Praha | UV Fluor. | 27 |
| | A | Brno | UV Fluor. | 16 |
| Denmark | A | Köbenhavn | KOM Imp. F. | 6-1 |
| Finland | A | Helsinki | UV Fluor./Cuol. | 2 |
| France | A | Paris | UV Fluor. | 7-40 |
| | B | Rouen | UV Fluor. | 3-9 |
| Germany | A | Berlin | .. | 39 |
| | A | München | .. | 5 |
| Greece | A | Athens | Pulsed fluor. | 5 |
| Hungary | A | Budapest | UV Fluor./W.Gaeke | 43 |
| | B | Miskolc | UV Fluor. | 8 |
| Iceland | A | Reykjavik | UV Fluor. | 1 |
| Luxemb. | A | Luxembourg | UV Fluor. | 2 |
| Norway | A | Oslo | Thorin/H2O2 | 2 |
| Poland | A | Lódz | Colorimetry | 19-12 |
| | C | Warszawa | Colorimetry | 8-6 |
| Portugal | A | Lisboa | UV Fluor. | 7 |
| Spain | A | Madrid | UV Fluor. | 14-10 |
| Sweden | A | Göteborg | UV Fluor. | 5-3 |
| | B | Stockholm | UV Fluor. | 5-2 |
| Switzerl. | A | Zurich | UV Fluor. c. | 1 |
| | B | Basel | UV Fluor. c. | 1 |
| Turkey | A | Ankara | H2O2/Conduct. | 7-8 |
| UK | A | London | Acid.Titr.c./UV Fluor. | 11 |
| | B | Newcastle | Acid. Titr. c. | 1 |

### NO2

| | Cat. (a) | City or area | Measurement method | No. Stn. (b) |
|---|---|---|---|---|
| Canada | A | Montreal | Chem. | 3 |
| | B | Hamilton | Chem. | 2 |
| Mexico | B | Mexico City | .. | 5 |
| USA | A | New York | Chem. | 3 |
| | A | Los Angeles | Chem. | 12 |
| Japan | A | Tokyo | Saltzman | 20-16 |
| | B | Kawasaki | Saltzman | 7-8 |
| Korea | A | Seoul | Chem. | 20 |
| | A | Pusan | Chem. | 7 |
| Austria | A | Wien | .. | 12 |
| | B | Linz | .. | 7 |
| Belgium | A | Bruxelles | Chem. c. | 4-6 |
| | B | Antwerpen | Chem. c. | 2-1 |
| Czech. R. | A | Praha | Chem. | 19-25 |
| | A | Brno | Chem. | 7-10 |
| Denmark | A | Köbenhavn | Chem. | 3-1 |
| Finland | A | Helsinki | Chem. | 2 |
| France | A | Paris | Chem. | 6-19 |
| | B | Rouen | Chem. | 3-6 |
| Germany | A | Berlin | .. | 5-21 |
| | A | München | .. | 5 |
| Greece | A | Athens | Chem. | 5 |
| Hungary | A | Budapest | Chem./Saltz. | 43 |
| | B | Miskolc | Chem. | 8 |
| Iceland | A | Reykjavik | Chem. | 1 |
| Luxemb. | A | Luxembourg | Chem. | 1 |
| Norway | A | Oslo | TGS abs. sol. | 1 |
| Poland | A | Lódz | Saltzman | 4-3 |
| | C | Warszawa | Saltzman | 3-2 |
| Portugal | A | Lisboa | Sod.Ars./Chem. | 1-11 |
| Spain | A | Madrid | Chem. | 6-14 |
| Sweden | A | Göteborg | Chem. c. | 1-3 |
| | B | Stockholm | Chem. c. | 2 |
| Switzerl. | A | Zurich | Chem. c. | 1 |
| | B | Basel | Chem. c. | 1 |
| Turkey | A | Ankara | Chem. | 2 |
| UK | A | London | Chem. c. | 1 |

(a)  Categories: A - city in which a notable portion (5-10%) of national population is concentrated; B - industrial city in which a significant number of inhabitants is considered to be exposed to the worst level of pollution in 1980; C - city with residential and service functions and with intermediate pollution level.

(b)  Number of monitoring stations may change over the years.

# WASTE

## MUNICIPAL WASTE

Data sources: OECD

- Municipal waste is waste collected by or on the order of municipalities. It includes waste originating from households (post-consumption waste), and similar waste from commerce and trade, office buildings, institutions (schools, hospitals, government buildings), and small businesses. It also includes waste from these sources collected door-to-door or delivered to the same facilities used for municipally collected waste, as well as fractions collected separately for recovery operations (through door-to-door collection and/or through voluntary deposit). Similar waste from rural areas, even if disposed of by the generator, is included. The definition also covers: (i) bulky waste (e.g. white goods, old furniture, mattresses); and (ii) yard waste, leaves, grass clippings, street sweepings, the contents of litter containers, and market cleansing waste, if managed as waste. The definition excludes waste from municipal sewage networks and treatment, as well as municipal construction and demolition waste. National definitions may differ.
- Values per capita are rounded.
- Change since 1980, italics: household waste only.
- Management of municipal waste: categories may overlap because residues from some types of treatment (incineration, composting) are landfilled; categories do not necessarily add up to 100% since other types of treatment may not be covered.

CAN  ➤  Data refer to 1992; municipal w.: all w. disposed of, except construction and demolition w., even if not collected by municipalities; includes flows diverted for recycling or composting.

MEX  ➤  Municipal w. and PFC data refer to 1996; household w. and management data refer to 1995; landfill: includes open landfill and illegal dumping.

USA  ➤  Data refer to 1995; landfill: after recovery and incineration.

JPN  ➤  Data refer to 1993.

KOR  ➤  Data refer to 1995.

AUS  ➤  1992 Secretariat estimate based on composite total from State/Territory data; may include significant amounts of commercial and industrial waste.

NZL  ➤  Data refer to 1995.

AUT  ➤  Data refer to 1993; municipal w.: excludes construction site w., which is included in national definition; data on management refer to hous. w. only.

BEL  ➤  Municipal w.: aggregate of 1995 data for Brussels and 1994 data for Flanders and Wallonia; data on management refer to Wallonia only; landfill: excludes residues from incineration and other operations.

CZE  ➤  Data refer to 1994; municipal w.: figure extrapolated from new survey; data on management refer to about 80% of municipal w. generated.

DNK  ➤  Data refer to 1995; municipal w. data come from a new survey done in treatment plants; data on management refer to household waste only.

FIN  ➤  Data refer to 1994; data on management are expert estimates and might include some w. from demolition sites and from sewerage and water treatment.

FRA  ➤  Data refer to 1993 and include DOM; municipal w.: includes 5 million tonnes of "Déchets industriels banals"; hous. w.: includes bulky w.

DEU  ➤  Data refer to 1993; municipal w. excludes separate collection for recycling purposes conducted outside the public sector (about 4.9 million tonnes in 1993); this particularly concerns packaging w. (paper, glass, metals, plastics) collected by the Duale System Deutschland; excludes w. directly brought to disposal sites by the generator and street cleaning w; change since 1980 of the private final consumption expenditure: western Germany only.

GRC  ➤  Data refer to 1992 traditional w. collection only.

HUN  ➤  Data refer to 1994; municipal w. refers to transported amounts; includes w. from households, offices, firms and services.

ISL  ➤  Data refer to 1994.

IRL  ➤  Data refer to 1995; management: recycling/composting: recycling only.

ITA  ➤  Data refer to 1995; municipal w. includes some w. from municipal sewage network and treatment.

LUX  ➤  Data refer to 1995 except for household w. which refers to 1992; municipal w.: excludes separate collection.

NLD  ➤  Municipal w. 1995; management: 1994; municipal w.: includes separate collection for recycling purposes, solid w. from sewerage and small amount of mixed building and construction w.; household w.: includes w. paper collected by schools, churches, sport clubs.

NOR  ➤  1995 figures based on a new survey covering all local authorities and treatment plants; it excludes a small amount of construction and demolition waste which was included in 1980.

POL  ➤  Data refer to 1995; management: recycling/composting: composting only.

PRT  ➤  Data refer to 1994.

ESP  ➤  Data refer to 1994.

SWE  ➤  Data refer to 1994; data on management refer to hous. w. only.

CHE  ➤  Data refer to 1996; municipal w.: includes separately collected waste for recycling (1.7 million tonnes).

TUR  ➤  1991 data based on daily amounts of w. collected in 1 974 municipalities out of a total of 2 033.

UKD  ➤  Data refer to 1995-96; household w.: incl. hous. hazardous w. and clinical w., street clean. w. and litter, w. taken to civic amenity sites for disposal or recycling; management: data related to 88% of households in England and Wales.

TOT  ➤  Rounded figures. Data do not include eastern Germany, Czech Rep., Hungary, Poland and Korea.

## INDUSTRIAL / NUCLEAR / HAZARDOUS WASTE

Data sources: OECD

- Industrial waste refers to waste generated by the manufacturing industry. National definitions often differ.
- Nuclear waste refers to spent fuel arisings in nuclear power plants. The data are expressed in tonnes of heavy metal. It should be noted that these data do not represent all radioactive waste generated.
- Hazardous waste refers to waste streams controlled according to the Basel Convention on Transboundary Movements of Hazardous Wastes and their Disposal (see Annex IV of the convention for complete definition and methods of treatment, movement and

disposal). National definitions often differ, and caution should be exercised when using these figures. Imports, exports: should refer to actual amounts moved, but may in some cases refer to total authorisations (notifications).

MEX  ➤  Ind. w.: 1990 data; haz. w.: 1995 production data refer to 1994.

USA  ➤  Haz. w.: movements: written notice and consent required for exports only.

JPN  ➤  Ind. w.: 1991; Nuc. w.: for fiscal year.

KOR  ➤  Ind. w.: 1995; Nuc. w.: Light Water Reactor fuel and Heavy Water Reactor fuel only.

AUS ➤ Ind. w.: refers to 1993 and to Queensland only; haz. w.: Victoria only.

NZL ➤ Haz. w.: production: 1990 data. Exports: for recovery only.

AUT ➤ Ind. w.: 1993. Austrian classification refers not to economic sectors but to waste streams. Data may not be comparable to those of other countries; haz. w.: data based on national law.

BEL ➤ Ind. w.: total based on Brussels 1992, Flanders 1994 and Wallonia 1994; haz. w.: production: notified amounts for Brussels and Wallonia; extrapolated amounts for Flanders. Movements: Wallonia and Flanders only; does not account for movements between regions.

CZE ➤ Ind. w.: 1994 data.

DNK ➤ Ind. w.: 1995 data; haz. w. according to the European Waste Catalogue.

FIN ➤ Ind. w.: 1992 estimates for dry weight based on wet weight figures; haz. w.: Ind. haz. w. only; data based on national law.

FRA ➤ Ind. w.: 1993 data. A detailed breakdown by ISIC sector is not available. Data may not be comparable to those of other countries; includes hazardous and non-hazardous w.; data may cover other ind. sectors; haz. w.: amount generated: all w. defined as special ind. w. in French legislation; no update available. Amounts to be managed: excludes internal treatment by private enterprises.

DEU ➤ Ind. w.: 1993 data; haz. w.: movements: w. going to final disposal only; data based on national law.

GRC ➤ Ind. w.: partial 1992 total; haz. w.: exports: PCB waste only.

HUN ➤ Ind. w.: 1994 data excluding haz. w.; waste from privatised enterprises may not be fully covered; haz. w.: according to Basel definition, haz. w. amounted to 2 306 kt in 1994.

ISL ➤ Ind. w.: 1994 data; mostly waste from slaughterhouses; haz. w.: excludes haz. w. from households and small enterprises.

IRL ➤ Ind. w.: 1995 data; haz. w.: data based on national law.

ITA ➤ Ind. w.: 1995 data; may include some mining & quarrying waste.

LUX ➤ Ind. w.: 1990 data for special industrial waste, mainly liquid waste assimilated in industrial waste water; haz. w.: data based on national law.

NLD ➤ Ind. w.: 1994 data; haz. w.: production: all waste defined as special waste in Dutch legislation. Haz. w. according to the Basel definition amounted to 575 kt in 1993.

NOR ➤ Ind. w.: 1993 data; haz. w.: production: all waste defined as special waste in Norwegian regulations. Data are estimates based on a special study carried out in 1995. If European Waste Catalogue relevant hazardous w. is included, production is 640 kt; movements: exclude aluminium salt slags (49 kt imported in 1993).

POL ➤ Ind. w.: 1995 data covering most industrial and energy sources; haz. w.: special waste, not fully consistent with Basel definition.

ESP ➤ Ind. w.: 1992 data.

SWE ➤ Ind. w.: rough estimates for 1993; sector specific waste.

CHE ➤ Ind. w.: 1995 data; haz. w.: all waste defined as special waste in Swiss legislation. Amount generated according to Basel Convention: 462 kt in 1993, 504 kt in 1994.

TUR ➤ Ind. w.: 1992 data.

UKD ➤ Ind. w.: includes 6 Mt from basic metal industries. The remaining 50 Mt is a broad estimate valid for any 12 month period in the late 1980s; haz. w.: refer to fiscal year. England and Wales only. Only waste going to final disposal must be notified (under 1988 transfrontier shipments of hazardous waste regulations). Total generated in UK: 2 077 kt in 1993/94.

TOT ➤ Ind. w.: rough Secretariat estimates.

## WASTE RECYCLING

Data sources: OECD, Fédération Européenne du Verre d'Emballage (Brussels), Confederation of European Paper Industries (Brussels), FAO

♦ Recycling is defined as reuse of material in a production process that diverts it from the waste stream, except for recycling within industrial plants and the reuse of material as fuel. The recycling rate is the ratio of the quantity recycled to the apparent consumption (domestic production + imports - exports).

♦ Table: data may refer to the years immediately preceding or following the columns' header; 1996: or latest available year; data prior to 1992 were not taken into account.

CAN ➤ Glass: packaging glass only.

MEX ➤ Recycling rates are based on amounts of waste generated.

USA ➤ Data refer to the material diverted from the municipal waste stream; recycling rates are based on amounts of waste generated.

JPN ➤ Glass: returnable bottles are excluded; data refer to reuse of glass as cullet compared to national production of glass bottles.

AUS ➤ Paper: data refer to newsprint, cardboard, and paper packaging; definitions of recycling vary according to the material collected (e.g. may include amounts incinerated to divert them from landfill).

BEL ➤ Paper: data for the latest year are estimates.

DEU ➤ 1980, 85, 90: western Germany; latest year: total Germany; glass: recycling rate is based on total sales.

GRC ➤ Amounts recycled exclude imports and exports.

ITA ➤ Glass: % of national production of glass containers for liquids.

NLD ➤ Paper: data refer to reuse in the paper industry only; glass: collected in bottle banks as % of sale on domestic market.

NOR ➤ Paper: collected amounts as % of apparent consumption; glass: excludes considerable amounts of glass recovered before entering the waste stream (deposit/reuse of bottles).

ESP ➤ Glass: collected amounts from household and industry as % of apparent consumption; include returnable bottles.

UKD ➤ Glass: Great Britain only; glass collected in bottle banks and from industrial sources (bottlers and packers) and flat glass.

# WATER QUALITY

## RIVER QUALITY

Data sources: OECD

♦ Measurement locations are at the mouth or downstream frontier of rivers.

♦ Data: refer to three year averages around 1980, 1985, 1990 and 1995, unless otherwise specified.

♦ Nitrates: Total concentrations unless otherwise specified.

MEX ➤ Lerma 1995: one year average (1994).

JPN ➤ 1995: one year average (1994).

AUT ➤ 1980: one year average.

FIN ➤ DO Kokemäenjoki 1995: one year average (1994). Nitrates Torniojoki 1980: one year average.

FRA ➤ Seine: station under marine influence. Rhône: since 1987 data refer to another station. Nitrates Loire and Seine: dissolved concentrations.

DEU ➤ Nitrates: Rhein, Donau: dissolved concentrations. Donau 1980 and 1985: one year average.

ITA ➤ Po: until 1988 data refer to Ponte Polesella (76 km from the mouth); since 1989 data refer to Pontelagoscuro (91 km from the mouth). DO 1995: one year average (1994).

LUX ➤ Moselle: 1980: one year average; DO 1985: one year average.

NLD ➤ Nitrates Maas-Keisersveer, Rijn-Lobith: dissolved concentr. Maas-Keisersveer 1995: one year average (1993).

POL ➢ 1980 and 1985: one year averages. Nysa Luzycka 1995: one year average (1993).
ESP ➢ Nitrates: dissolved concentrations.
CHE ➢ 1995: one year average (1994).

## WASTE WATER TREATMENT

Data sources:     OECD

◆ Total served: national population connected to public sewage treatment plants. Includes: primary treatment - physical and mechanical processes which result in decanted effluents and separate sludge (sedimentation, flotation, etc.); secondary treatment - biological treatment technologies, i.e. processes which employ anaerobic or aerobic micro-organisms; tertiary treatment - advanced treatment technologies, i.e. chemical processes.
◆ Sewerage connection rates: refers to population connected to public sewage network with or without treatment.
◆ Mid-1990s: data refer to 1995 unless otherwise specified. Data prior to 1993 have not been considered.
CAN ➢ Data refer to 1981 and 1994. Secondary usually includes private treatment & waste stabilisation ponds. Tertiary: secondary with phosphorus removal.
MEX ➢ 1995: 1993 data.
USA ➢ Data refer to 1982. Primary: may include ocean outfalls and some biological treatment. Tertiary: includes 2-3% of non-discharge treatment, e.g. lagoons, evaporation ponds. Excludes rural areas served by on-site disposal systems.
JPN ➢ 1995: 1993 data. Secondary: may include primary treatment and some tertiary treatment.
KOR ➢ 1995: 1994 data.
BEL ➢ 1995: Secretariat estimates.
DNK ➢ 1995: 1994 data.

## PUBLIC EXPENDITURE ON WATER

Data sources:     OECD

◆ Data refer to public pollution abatement and control (PAC) expenditure (see Expenditure item) at current prices and purchasing power parities for the latest available year. PAC activities for soil and water comprise collection and purification of waste water, combating of pollution in the marine environment, prevention, control and monitoring of surface water pollution, combating of pollution of inland surface waters, prevention and combating of thermal pollution of water, abatement of groundwater and soil pollution, and regulation and monitoring. Excludes the

UKD ➢ Nitrates: when the parameter is unmeasurable (quantity too small) the limit of detection values are used when calculating annual averages. Actual averages may therefore be lower. Mersey 1980: one year average.

FIN ➢ Secondary: 50-80% removal of BOD; tertiary: 70-90% removal of BOD. 1995: 1993 data.
FRA ➢ 1980 : Secretariat estimates. 1995 (1994 data): in % of dwellings, which is considered a good estimate of the population connected.
DEU ➢ 1980 data refer to 1979. Until 1985 data refer to w. Germany only.
HUN ➢ 1995: 1993 data.
NLD ➢ 1980 and 1995: 1981 and 1994 data. Tertiary: includes dephosphatation and/or disinfection.
PRT ➢ 1980 : 1981 data.
SWE ➢ Primary: may include removal of sediments. Secondary: chemical or biological treatment. Tertiary: chemical and biological plus complementary treatment.
TUR ➢ Data result from an inventory covering municipalities with an urban population of over 3 000, assuming that the sewerage system and treatment facilities serve the whole population of the municipalities.
UKD ➢ 1994 data: England and Wales only; data refer to financial year (April to March). Subtotals may not add up to the totals due to rounding. Primary: removal of gross solids. Secondary: removal of organic material or bacteria under aerobic conditions. Tertiary: removal of suspended solids following secondary treatment.
TOT ➢ Secretariat estimates, not taking into account Australia. 1980: include w. Germany only; data cover 23 OECD Member countries (Mexico, Korea, Australia, Czech Rep., Hungary and Poland were not taken into account).

supply of drinking water.
CAN ➢ Expenditure: according to the financing principle; estimated 1994 data.
KOR ➢ Trial estimate by the Bank of Korea.
BEL ➢ Data do not include Brussels; figures refer to regional administrations only; federal and local (municipalities and provinces) administrative levels are excluded.
FIN ➢ Data refer to municipalities only.
DEU ➢ 1993 data for western Germany only.
SWE ➢ Data refer to municipalities only.

# WATER RESOURCES

## INTENSITY OF USE OF WATER RESOURCES

Data sources:     OECD, FAO, World Resources Institute (WRI)

◆ Abstractions: accounts for total water withdrawal without deducting water that is reintroduced into the natural environment after use.
◆ Abstractions as % of available resources: data refer to total abstraction divided by total renewable resources, except for totals, where the internal resource estimates were used to avoid double counting.
◆ Renewable water resources: net result of precipitation minus evapo-transpiration (internal) plus inflow (total). This definition ignores differences in storage capacity, and represents the maximum quantity of fresh water available on average.
◆ Inflow: water flows from neighbouring countries. Includes underground flows.
◆ Water stress (source: CSD, "Comprehensive Assessment of the Freshwater Resources of the World") is based on the ratio of water withdrawal to annual water availability.

◆ Low (less than 10 per cent ): generally there is no major stress on the available resources.
◆ Moderate (10 to 20 per cent): indicates that water availability is becoming a constraint on development and significant investments are needed to provide adequate supplies.
◆ Medium-high (20 to 40 per cent): implies the management of both supply and demand, and conflicts among competing uses need to be resolved.
◆ High (more than 40 per cent): indicates serious scarcity, and usually shows unsustainable water use, which can become a limiting factor in social and economic development.
National water stress levels may hide important variations at subnational (e.g. river basin) level; in particular in countries with extensive arid and semi-arid regions.
◆ Freshwater abstractions by major sector
  ◆ "Public water supply" refers to water supply by waterworks, and may include other uses besides the domestic sector.

◆ "Irrigation" refers to self supply (abstraction for own final use). "Others": include industry and electrical cooling (self supply).

◆ Freshwater abstractions data: refers to 1995 or latest available year (data prior to 1987 have not been considered).

◆ <u>Cultivated land:</u> refers to arable and permanent crop land.

CAN ➢ 1980 and Mid-1990s: 1981 and 1991 data.

MEX ➢ Data include Secretariat estimates for electrical cooling - 1980: based on electricity generation in power stations; 1995: based on 1994 data.

USA ➢ Mid-1990s: 1990 data.

JPN ➢ Mid-1990s: Secretariat estimates based on 1990 and 1994 data.

KOR ➢ Partial totals excluding electrical cooling. Mid-1990s: 1994 data.

AUS ➢ In Australia the intensity of use of water resources varies widely among regions; one third of the country is arid, one third semi-arid and the high rainfall areas in the north are far from the densily populated areas in the south. 1980: 1977 data adjusted for an average climatic year. Mid-1990s: estimated data.

NZL ➢ Partial totals excluding industrial and electrical cooling. 1980: composite total based on data for various years. Mid-1990s: 1993 estimates.

AUT ➢ Partial totals. Irrigation and industry no cooling: groundwater only. Electrical cooling (includes all industrial cooling): surface water only. Mid-1990s: 1993 data.

BEL ➢ Data include Secretariat estimates.

CZE ➢ Data refer to 1996.

DNK ➢ 1980: 1977 data. Latest y.: groundwater only, represents the major part of total freshwater abstractions (e.g. 95-99% for 1995).

FIN ➢ Partial totals. Mid-1990s: 1994 data excluding all agricultural uses.

FRA ➢ 1980 and Mid-1990s: 1981 and 1994 data. Irrigation: Secretariat estimates; includes other agricultural uses, but irrigation is the main use.

DEU ➢ Excluding agricultural uses other than irrigation. Mid-1990s: 1995 provisional data which include 1991 data for irrigation; as abstractions for irrigation have significantly decreased since 1991, data represent an overestimation. Change since 1980: western Germany only; referring to 1980-91.

HUN ➢ Mid-1990s: 1994 data.

**WATER PRICE**

Data sources: IWSA (International Water Supply Association), 1997, International Statistics for Water Supply

◆ Prices calculated on the basis of a family of four (two adults and two children) living in a house with garden rather than an apartment. Where there are water meters, the price is based on annual consumption of 200 m³. Where supply is normally unmeasured the average price has been used (Norway and UK).

ISL ➢ After 1985, fish farming is a major user of abstracted water.

IRE ➢ Mid-1990s: 1994 data; totals include 1980 data for electrical cooling.

ITA ➢ Excluding agricultural uses besides irrigation. 1980: including 1973 estimates for industrial cooling. Mid-1990s: 1987 data.

LUX ➢ Mid-1990s: annual average of the 1990-95 period.

NLD ➢ Partial totals excluding all agricultural uses. 1980 and Mid-1990s: 1981 and 1991 data.

POL ➢ Totals include abstractions for agriculture, which include aquaculture (areas over 10 ha) and irrigation (arable land and forest areas greater than 20 ha); animal production and domestic needs of rural inhabitants are not covered.

PRT ➢ Mid-1990s: 1991 data.

ESP ➢ Excluding agricultural uses other than irrigation. Groundwater: excluding industry except for 1995. Mid-1990s: hydrological year average, except for electrical cooling (1995 data).

SWE ➢ 1980: include data from different years.

CHE ➢ Partial totals excluding all agricultural uses. Mid-1990s: 1994 data.

TUR ➢ 1980: partial totals; excluding agricultural uses other than irrigation and electrical cooling.

UKD ➢ Partial totals. England and Wales only. Mid-1990s: 1994 data. Data include miscellaneous uses for power generation, but exclude hydroelectric power water use.

TOT ➢ Rounded figures, including Secretariat estimates. OECD % change (water abstractions): western Germany only. % of renewable resources: calculated using the estimated totals for internal resources (not total resources as for countries), and considering England and Wales only.

IRRIGATION

JPN ➢ Rice irrigation only.

KOR ➢ Rice irrigation only.

BEL ➢ Data for Belgium include Luxembourg.

DNK ➢ Land provided with irrigation facilities only.

FIN ➢ Land provided with irrigation facilities only.

FRA ➢ Land provided with irrigation facilities only.

HUN ➢ Data exclude complementary farm plots and individual farms.

TUR ➢ Includes meadows and pastures (about 10 per cent of total).

UKD ➢ England and Wales only.

Prices at current exchange rates. VAT is not included.

NZL ➢ Secretariat estimates based on water meter charges for the 1997/98 fiscal year, and considering an annual consumption of 200 m³.

DEU ➢ Country data which refer to 1997 and are provisional.

NOR ➢ Unmeasured data: refer to the average price.

UKD ➢ Unmeasured data: refer to the average price.

# FOREST RESOURCES

**INTENSITY OF USE OF FOREST RESOURCES**

Data sources: OECD, FAO, national statistical yearbooks

◆ <u>Annual growth:</u> gross increment.

◆ Mid-1990s: 1995 or latest available year.

◆ Data exclude Iceland as there is no traditional forestry in this country.

CAN ➢ Growth: refers to Canada's definition of "allowable annual cut". Mid-1990s: 1994 data.

USA ➢ Under bark volumes. Concerns timberland with annual production greater than 20 cubic feet per acre (about 66% of total forest land). Growth: excludes natural forests. Mid-1990s: 1990 data.

JPN ➢ 1980s: 1985 data. Growth: national forest; 1995 data: Basic Plan for Forest Resources.

KOR ➢ Annual harvest % change since 1980: refer to 1980-90.

AUT ➢ Mid-1990s: 1990 data. Growth: 1980 data refer to 1971-80.

BEL ➢ Wallonia only. 1980s: 1985 data. Mid-1990s: include Secretariat estimates (based on 1992 data for annual growth).

DNK ➢ 1980 data are Secretariat estimates. Growth Mid-1990s (1994 data): expected mean annual volume increment for 1990-2000.

FRA ➢ Harvers: includes fuelwood and charcoal. Data refer to production forest only.

GRC ➢ Mid-1990s: 1992 data.

ITA  ➤ Mid-1990s: 1992 data.
LUX  ➤ 1980s: 1985 data. Mid-1990s: include Secretariat estimates (based on 1992 data for annual growth).
NLD  ➤ Data refer to total exploitable forest. 1980s: 1985 data.
PRT  ➤ Mid-1990s: 1990 data.
ESP  ➤ Growth 1980: Secretariat estimates.
SWE  ➤ 1980 data refer to 1971-80. Mid-1990s: harvest data refer to 1991-94, and annual growth to 1993-94.
CHE  ➤ Mid-1990s: 1996 data.
TUR  ➤ Mid-1990s: 1990 data.
UKD  ➤ Mid-1990s: 1990 data.
OECD ➤ Secretariat estimates; excludes eastern Germany and Korea.

GROWING STOCK

- Data include exploitable and non-exploitable forests.
- Data refer to 1995 or latest year available.

**FOREST AND WOODED LAND**

Data sources:  OECD, FAO

- Data include Secretariat estimates.
CAN  ➤ Numerical differences between successive national inventories do not necessarily reflect real changes. Accordingly forest in Canada has been considered as constant, taking into account the most recent figure available (1991).
MEX  ➤ Excl. vegetation in arid areas, hydrophilic and halophilic vegetation and affected forest areas included in forest inventory.
USA  ➤ Forest land with annual production > 20 cubic feet per acre. 1995: 1992 data.
JPN  ➤ Areas under the management of the Ministry of Forestry.
NZL  ➤ 1995: 1992 data.
AUS  ➤ Data are approximations.
AUT  ➤ 1970, 1980, 1990 and 1995 data refer to 1961-70, 1971-80, 1986-90; exploitable forests only.
BEL  ➤ Change in data source between 1970 and 1980.

CAN  ➤ % change since 1980: refer to 1981-1991. Growing stock: the increase from 1981 reflects changes in methodology, increases in the extent of the land base that is covered by the inventory as well as growth.
MEX  ➤ 1980: Secretariat estimates.
USA  ➤ Under bark excluded. Productive off-reserve forests only.
FIN  ➤ National Forest Inventory data for 1989-94.
DEU  ➤ Western Germany only; data include estimates.
LUX  ➤ % change since 1980: refer to 1985-1995.
NLD  ➤ % change since 1980: refer to 1985-1995.
POL  ➤ State on 1 January 1995.
SWE  ➤ Latest available year: data refer to 1993-94.
OECD ➤ Secretariat estimates; includes western Germany only.

FORESTRY PRODUCTS AS % OF NATIONAL EXPORTS OF GOODS

BEL  ➤ Belgium and Luxembourg.
LUX  ➤ Belgium and Luxembourg.

DNK  ➤ Change in definition in wooded area; comparison requires caution. Accordingly 1990 and 1995 data are Secretariat estimates referring to 1976 data.
FIN  ➤ 1995 figures are based on National Forest Inventory 1989-94. Includes all the wooded land where the annual potential wood production exceeds 0.1 m3/ha.
DEU  ➤ 1995: 1993 data; forest and woodland on holdings of 1 hectare and above, and on holdings of less than 1 hectare whose production market values exceed a fixed minimum.
GRC  ➤ According to 1992 inventory: 65 130 km² (figure considered for most recent year is 26 200 km²).
ISL  ➤ Data refer to land outside agricultural areas.
ITA  ➤ Since 1986 some agricultural land has been reclassified as forest land; since 1990 Mediterranean maquis have been included in mixed forest.
LUX  ➤ Inventory methodology changed between 1980 and 1990.
NLD  ➤ 1980, 1990 and 1995 data refer to 1979, 1989 and 1993.
TOT  ➤ Include Secretariat estimates.

# FISH RESOURCES

**FISH CATCHES AND CONSUMPTION**

Data sources:  FAO

- Total catches: data refer to capture fisheries in inland and marine waters, including freshwater fish, diadromous fish, marine fish, crustaceans, molluscs and miscellaneous aquatic animals; excludes aquaculture.
- Marine catches: include marine fish, crustaceans, and molluscs.
- World marine fish resources by phase of fishery development: the figure illustrates the process of intensification of fisheries since 1950 and the increase in the proportion of world resources which are subject to declines in productivity. The resources refer to the top 200 species-area combinations for marine fish, selected for analysis on the basis of average landings over the whole time period. These 200 major resources account for 77% of world marine fish production.

  The process of development of a fishery is schematically represented in the figure next column:

  The relative rate of increase during the development process, which varies significantly as the maximum long-term yield is approached, reached and "overshot" has been used here to provide a rough assessment of the state of marine resources.

  For further details, please refer to: "Review of the state of world fishery resources: marine fisheries", FAO, Rome 1997.

- Fish consumption: Total food supply = production - non-food use + imports - exports + stock variations. Data refer to 1995 or latest available year; totals refer to 1993.

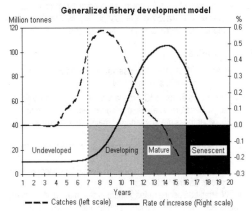

**Generalized fishery development model**

BEL  ➤ Data include Luxembourg.
DNK  ➤ Excludes Greenland and Faroe Islands.

# BIODIVERSITY

## THREATENED SPECIES

Data sources:   OECD

♦ Threatened species: "Threatened" refers to the sum of the number of species in the "endangered" and "vulnerable" categories.

♦ "Endangered": species in danger of extinction and whose survival is unlikely if the causal factors continue operating.

♦ "Vulnerable": species believed likely to move into the "endangered" category in the near future if the causal factors continue operating.

♦ When interpreting these tables, it should be borne in mind that the number of species known does not always accurately reflect the number of species in existence; and that the definitions are applied with varying degrees of rigour in countries, although international organisations such as the IUCN and the OECD are promoting standardisation.

CAN ➢ Indigenous species only; all reptile and amphibian species are declining somewhat due to urbanisation and agriculture.

MEX ➢ Excludes extinct species; birds: resident and migratory species; fish: freshwater and marine species.

USA ➢ Including Pacific and Caribbean islands.

JPN ➢ Mammals: of which 179 indigenous species; birds: includes species that are occasionally present; fish: freshwater and brackish water species; reptiles, amphibians: of which 86 and 56 indigenous species.

KOR ➢ Excludes extinct species; fish: freshwater only (825 marine species are known).

NZL ➢ Data refer to indigenous species only (many species have been introduced, most classed as noxious); mammals: land-breeding mammals only (data refer to two species of bats and three species of pinnipeds, all threatened); cetaceans are excluded (their population status is often uncertain); fish: freshwater only.

AUT ➢ Threatened mammals: includes extinct and/or vanished species; birds: breeding species on national territory; fish: freshwater only.

BEL ➢ Data refer to Flanders; extinct species are excluded.

CZE ➢ Data refer to indigenous species.

DNK ➢ Fish: freshwater only; known species of vascular plants: indigenous species only.

FIN ➢ Excludes extinct species; mammals: indigenous species only; fish: excl. introduced species and occasionally present marine fish.

FRA ➢ Metropolitan France; extinct species are excluded; mammals: of which 112 indigenous species; birds: number of breeding pairs; fish: marine and freshwater species.

DEU ➢ Mammals: of which 83 indigenous species; birds: breeding species, of which 257 indigenous species; fish: freshwater only; reptiles and amphibians: indigenous species.

GRC ➢ Fish: freshwater only; no marine species are threatened; 1993 data; vascular plants, threatened: incl. eight extinct species.

HUN ➢ Threatened: protected and highly protected species; birds: of which 212 indigenous species; fish: freshwater species, of which 2 indigenous species; "Threatened" fish: includes indeterminate species; vascular plants: of which 2 433 indigenous species.

ISL ➢ Birds: breeding species only; fish: freshwater only; vascular plants: data refer to 1996 official Red List for plants elaborated according to the 1995 IUCN criteria; therefore, the "threatened" category is stricter than for other countries.

ITA ➢ Fish: freshwater only.

NLD ➢ Excl. extinct species; birds: breeding species only; fish: freshwater only.

NOR ➢ Excludes extinct species; mammals: indigenous terrestrial species; the status of the 26 known species of marine mammals is uncertain; birds: breeding species on national territory; reptiles and amphibians: indigenous species; vascular plants: native species only; 2 492 species (incl. introduced ones) are known.

POL ➢ Mammals: indigenous species only (out of 90 species); birds: breeding species only (total number of species recorded so far in Poland: 418); fish: freshwater indigenous species, excluding lampreys (out of 66 freshwater species); vascular plants: of which 1 950 indigenous species.

PRT ➢ Fish: freshwater species only.

ESP ➢ Fish: freshwater species only.

SWE ➢ Mammals, birds: of which 60, 243 indigenous species.

CHE ➢ Mammals: indigenous species; birds: all breeding species on national territory; fish: indigenous species of Pisces and Cyclostomata; reptiles and amphibians: indigenous species.

TUR ➢ Birds: regularly breeding species (out of 450 species known).

UKD ➢ Great Britain only; mammals: terrestrial and marine species, excluding cetaceans; 41 of species known are native; "threatened" refers to national standard; birds: total number of native species recorded in Britain and Ireland on the British Ornithologists' Union list A; these include 237 regularly breeding species and 54 common passage migrants and winter visitors; fish (of which 37 indigenous): freshwater fish, including those that leave the sea to breed in fresh water (e.g. salmon); reptiles and amphibians: indigenous species; vascular plants, species known: includes 800 microspecies.

## PROTECTED AREAS

Data sources:   OECD, World Conservation Monitoring Centre provisional data, IUCN

♦ Major protected areas: IUCN management categories I-VI:
  ♦ Ia: strict nature reserves, managed mainly for science;
  ♦ Ib: wilderness areas, managed mainly for wilderness protection;
  ♦ II: national parks, managed mainly for ecosystem protection and recreation;
  ♦ III: natural monuments, managed mainly for conservation of specific natural features;
  ♦ IV: habitat/species management areas, managed mainly for habitat and species conservation through management intervention;
  ♦ V: protected landscapes/seascapes, managed mainly for landscape/seascape conservation and recreation;
  ♦ VI: managed resource protected areas, managed mainly for the sustainable use of natural ecosystems.

♦ For further details on management categories please refer to "Guidelines for Protected Area Management Categories", IUCN, 1994.

♦ See also the Recommendations established at the IVth World Congress on National Parks and Protected Areas.

♦ National classifications may differ. Includes only areas greater than 10 km$^2$ or completely protected islands of more than 1 km$^2$.

MEX ➢ As of 1997 there were 107 national protected areas under the National System of Natural Protected Areas (SINAP), with a total size of 117 340 km$^2$.

USA ➢ Includes Alaska: 104 protected areas totalling 745 390 km$^2$. Excludes American Samoa, Guam, minor outlying islands, Puerto Rico and Virgin Islands.

AUS ➢ 1997 national data; excludes the Great Barrier Reef Marine Park totalling 344 800 km$^2$ (cat. VI).

DNK ➢ Excludes Greenland: one national park of 972 000 km$^2$.

FRA ➢ Excludes non-metropolitan France.

NLD ➢ Excludes the Netherlands Antilles.

NOR ➤ Includes Svalbard, Jan Mayen and Bouvet islands: 10 protected
     areas totalling 72 920 km².
PRT ➤ Includes Azores and Madeira (respectively, 6 and 4 sites totalling
     482 km² and 413 km²).

ESP ➤ Includes Baleares and Canaries (respectively, 3 and 45 sites
     totalling 1 674 km² and 2 905 km²).

## GDP AND POPULATION

### GROSS DOMESTIC PRODUCT

Data sources: OECD.

- Gross Domestic Product: expressed at 1991 price levels and
  purchasing power parities.
- Value added: Mid-1990s: 1995 or latest available year;
  agriculture: also includes hunting, forestry and fishing; industry:
  includes mining and quarrying, manufacturing, gas, electricity and
  water, and construction (ISIC 2 through 5); services: includes
  import duties and other adjustments; excludes imputed bank
  service charges.

DEU ➤ % change GDP - % change population and structure of GDP:
     refer to western Germany only.
HUN ➤ Value added: as % of total of branches at basic prices.
POL ➤ Value added: as % of total of branches at basic prices.
TOT ➤ % change GDP - % change population and structure of GDP:
     includes western Germany only; % change GDP - % change
     population: excludes Czech Republic, Hungary and Poland.

### POPULATION GROWTH AND DENSITY

Data sources: OECD

- Population: all nationals present in or temporarily absent from a
  country, and aliens permanently settled in the country.

- Unemployment rate: commonly used definitions.
ISL ➤ Registered unemployment.

## CONSUMPTION

### PRIVATE FINAL CONSUMPTION EXPENDITURE

Data sources: OECD

- Private final consumption expenditure: the sum of (i) the outlays of
  resident households on new durable and non-durable goods and
  services less their net sales of second-hand goods, scraps and
  wastes; (ii) the value of goods and services produced by private
  non-profit institutions for own use on current account; expressed at

1991 price levels and purchasing power parities. Consumption
patterns: data refer to 1995 or 1994.
DEU ➤ Change since 1980 and consumption pattern refer to western
     Germany only.
TOT ➤ Change since 1980: includes western Germany only and excludes
     Czech Republic, Hungary and Poland.

### GOVERNMENT FINAL CONSUMPTION EXPENDITURE

Data sources: OECD

- Government final consumption expenditure: the value of goods
  and services produced by governments for their own use on
  current account; expressed at 1991 price levels and purchasing
  power parities.

DEU ➤ Change since 1980 refers to western Germany only.
TOT ➤ Change since 1980: includes western Germany only and excludes
     Czech Republic, Hungary and Poland.

## ENERGY

### ENERGY SUPPLY

Data sources: IEA-OECD

- see IEA (1994-95) *Energy Balances of OECD Countries* for
  conversion factors from original units to Toe for the various energy
  sources.

- Total primary energy supply: indigenous production + imports -
  exports - international marine bunkers and ± stock changes.
  Primary energy comprises hard coal, lignite and other solid fuels,
  crude oil and natural gas liquids, natural gas, and nuclear, hydro,
  geothermal and solar electricity. Electricity trade is also included.
- Solid fuels: coal, combustible renewables and waste.

### ENERGY PRICES AND TAXES

Data sources: IEA-OECD

- see IEA (1997) "Energy prices and taxes, third quarter, 1997"
- Oil: light fuel oil only.
- Oil and electricity: US$ using current exchange rates.
- Natural gas: US$ per 10⁷ kcal (GCV basis) using current exchange
  rates.

- Real energy end-use prices: refers to real energy end-use prices
  for industry and households. % change refer to 1980-96 period.
MEX ➤ Energy prices: % change refer to 1982-96 period.
ISL ➤ National data which may differ from those of other OECD
     countries; industry: medium price for power-intensive industries
     and other industries.
NOR ➤ Electricity for industry refers to 1991.

# TRANSPORT

## ROAD TRAFFIC

Data sources:  OECD, International Road Federation (IRF), national yearbooks

♦ Traffic volumes are expressed in billions of kilometres travelled by road vehicle; they are usually estimates and represent the average annual distance covered by vehicles, in kilometres, multiplied by the number of vehicles in operation. In principle, the data refer to the whole distance travelled on the whole network inside the national boundaries by national vehicles, with exception of two- and three-wheeled vehicles, caravans, and trailers.

♦ Data include Secretariat estimates.

USA ➤ Traffic by local and urban buses is excluded.
JPN ➤ Traffic by light vehicles is excluded.
FRA ➤ Traffic by buses of the Régie Autonome des Transports Parisiens is excluded.

## MOTOR VEHICLES

Data sources:  OECD, European Conference of Ministers of Transport (ECMT), IRF, American Automobile Manufacturers' Association, national yearbooks

♦ Total stock includes passenger cars, goods vehicles, buses and coaches. Data refer to autonomous road vehicles with four or more wheels, excluding caravans and trailers, military vehicles, special vehicles (for emergency services, construction machinery, etc.) and agricultural tractors.

♦ Private car ownership is expressed as passenger cars per capita. Data refer to passenger cars seating not more than nine persons

## ROAD INFRASTRUCTURE

Data sources:  OECD, ECMT, IRF, national yearbooks

♦ Roads refer to motorways, main or national highways, secondary or regional roads, and others. In principle, the data refer to all public roads, streets and paths in urban and rural areas, but not private roads.

♦ Motorways refer to a class of roads differing from main or national, secondary or regional, and other roads.

♦ Data describe the situation as of 31 December of the year.

♦ Data include Secretariat estimates.

MEX ➤ Motorways refer to toll roads.
AUS ➤ Road network: road types taken into account changed in 1982 and 1985.
AUT ➤ Road network: about 100 000 km of private roads are included.

## ROAD FUEL PRICES AND TAXES

Data sources:  IEA-OECD

♦ see IEA (1997), *Energy Prices and Taxes, Third Quarter*
♦ Taxes:  includes taxes that have to be paid by the consumer as part of the transaction and are not refundable.
♦ Diesel fuel:  diesel for commercial use.
♦ Unleaded gasoline:  unleaded premium (95 RON) except as noted.
♦ Prices:  expressed in US$ at 1991 prices and PPPs.
♦ Total energy consumption by road traffic:  all fuels used in road vehicles (including military) as well as agricultural and industrial highway use; excludes gasoline used in stationary engines, and diesel oil in tractors that are not for highway use.

CAN ➤ Diesel: 1980 data refer to 1981. Unleaded gasoline: unleaded regular (92 RON).
MEX ➤ Unleaded gasoline: unleaded regular (92 RON).

wDEU ➤ Except for caravans and large trailers hauled by passenger-carrying vehicles, traffic by special vehicles is included.
GRC ➤ Data refer to inter-city traffic only.
ISL ➤ Traffic by local and urban buses is excluded. Traffic intensity per network length is with respect to major roads and secondary roads ( 8 181 km in 1995).
ITA ➤ Traffic by three-wheeled goods vehicles is included.
NLD ➤ Traffic by trams and subways is included.
ESP ➤ Data refer only to traffic on motorways and national roads.
SWE ➤ Data include traffic by Swedish passenger cars abroad. Traffic by goods vehicles with a load capacity under 2 tonnes is excluded. Up to 1988, only the public network is included; after 1989, the total network is taken into account.
TUR ➤ Data refer only to traffic on motorways and national roads.
UKD ➤ Data refer to Great Britain only.

(including the driver), including rental cars, taxis, jeeps, estate cars/station wagons and similar light, dual-purpose vehicles.
♦ Data describe the situation as of 31 December of the year.
JPN ➤ Total stocks include three-wheeled vehicles.
AUS ➤ Private car ownership includes utility vehicles.
BEL ➤ Data are reported on 1 August of the reference year.
FRA ➤ Data are reported on 1 January.
DEU ➤ Total stocks include tractors.
LUX ➤ Data are reported on 1 January of the reference year.
NLD ➤ Data are reported on 31 July of the reference year.
CHE ➤ Data are reported on 30 September of the reference year.
UKD ➤ Total stocks include special purpose vehicles.

FIN ➤ Road network: urban streets are excluded.
FRA ➤ Road network: excludes certain rural roads (700 000 km in 1987). Motorways include about 1 200 km of urban motorways.
GRC ➤ Road network: excl. other roads (estim. at 75 600 km in 1995).
ESP ➤ Road network: motorways, national and secondary roads only. Excludes other roads estimated at 175 000 km in 1995. Motorways: certain two-lane roads are included.
SWE ➤ Road network: private roads are excluded. Motorways: excludes access and exit ramps.
TUR ➤ Road network: national and provincial roads only. Village roads are excluded (320 055 km in 1995).
UKD ➤ Data refer to Great Britain only. Motorways: excl. slip roads.

USA ➤ Unleaded gasoline: 1980 data refer to 1981.
JPN ➤ Unleaded gasoline: unleaded regular (91 RON).
KOR ➤ 1980 data refer to 1981.
AUS ➤ Diesel: 1985 data refer to 1986.
NZL ➤ Unleaded gasoline: unleaded regular (91 RON).
DNK ➤ Unleaded gasoline: unleaded premium (98 RON).
FIN ➤ Diesel: 1985 data refer to 1986.
FRA ➤ Up to February 1985 prices were kept within a set range. Figures before 1985 refer to maximum price for Paris. Figures after 1985 refer to average price for all of France.
wDEU ➤ Unleaded gasoline: 1985 data refer to 1986.
ISL ➤ Data from Statistics Iceland.
NOR ➤ Unleaded gasoline: 1985 data refer to 1986.
CHE ➤ Unleaded gasoline: 1985 data refer to 1986.

# AGRICULTURE

## INTENSITY OF USE FROM NITROGEN AND PHOSPHATE FERTILISERS

Data sources:   OECD, FAO, International Fertilizer Industry Association, national statistical yearbooks, UN/ECE, UNEP

- Use of nitrogen and phosphate fertilisers: data refer to the nitrogen (N) and phosphoric acid (P2O5) content of commercial fertilisers, and relate to apparent consumption during the fertiliser year (generally 1 July to 30 June) per unit of agricultural land.
- Agricultural land: refers to arable and permanent crop land and permanent grassland. "Arable l." refers to all land generally under rotation, whether for temporary crops or meadows, or left fallow. "Permanent crops l." comprises those lands occupied for a long period that do not have to be planted for several years after each harvest. "Permanent grassland" includes land used for five years or more for herbaceous forage, either cultivated or growing wild.
- Data includes estimates.
- Phosphate fert.: includes ground rock phosphates.

MEX   ➢ Fertiliser year: calendar year.
USA   ➢ Includes data for Puerto Rico.
KOR   ➢ Fertiliser year: calendar year.
BEL   ➢ Data for Belgium include Luxembourg.
           Phosphate fert.: excludes other citrate soluble phosphates.
DNK   ➢ Fertiliser year: August-July.
FRA   ➢ Phosphate fert.: fertiliser year: May-April.
GRC   ➢ Fertiliser year: calendar year.
HUN   ➢ Fertiliser year: calendar year.
ISL   ➢ Fertiliser year: calendar year.

## LIVESTOCK DENSITIES

Data sources:   OECD, FAO, UN/ECE

| Coefficients used to estimate nitrogen from livestock | | |
|---|---|---|
| | kg of dry matter per year | Coefficients for N content in excrement (% of dry matter) |
| Cattle | 1 500 | 5.0 |
| Horses | 1 200 | 4.4 |
| Sheep and goats | 250 | 3.0 |
| Pigs | 250 | 4.4 |
| Poultry (hens) | 15 | 5.3 |

Source: IEDS-UN/ECE

BEL   ➢ Data for Belgium include Luxembourg.
CZE   ➢ Sheep and goats: sheep only.

## INTENSITY OF USE OF PESTICIDES

Data sources:   OECD, FAO, national statistical yearbooks, European Crop Protection Association

- Unless otherwise specified, data refer to active ingredients.
- Unless otherwise specified, data refer to total consumption of pesticides, which include: insecticides (acaricides, molluscicides and nematocides), fungicides (bactericides and seed treatments), herbicides (defoliants and desiccants), and other pesticides (plant growth regulators and rodenticides).

CAN   ➢ Survey coverage has varied greatly (different active ingredients, registrants and products); survey trends may therefore not reflect actual trends but simply changes in the survey coverage. 1994: refer to agriculture uses only (non-agricultural uses excluded). % change since 1980: base year refer to 1984.
JPN   ➢ Data refer to national production of pesticides.
KOR   ➢ % change since 1980: base year refer to 1986.
NZL   ➢ % change since 1980: base year refer to 1985.
BEL   ➢ Data include Luxembourg.

ESP   ➢ Fertiliser year: calendar year.
SWE   ➢ Fertiliser year: June-May. Nitrogen fert.: data include forest fertilisation.
TUR   ➢ Fertiliser year: calendar year.
UKD   ➢ Fertiliser year: June-May.

## AGRICULTURAL PRODUCTION

Data sources:   OECD, FAO

- Data refer to indices of agricultural production based on price-weighted quantities of agricultural commodities produced for any use except as seed and feed. The commodities covered are all crops and livestock products originating in each country.
- Data may differ from national data due to differences in concepts of production, coverage, weights, time reference and methods of calculation.

BEL   ➢ Data for Belgium include Luxembourg.

## AGRICULTURAL VALUE ADDED

Data sources:   OECD

- Data also includes hunting, forestry and fishing.
- Data refer to 1995 or latest year available.

DEU   ➢ Value added: western Germany only.
HUN   ➢ Value added: as % of total of branches at basic prices.
POL   ➢ Value added: as % of total of branches at basic prices.
TOT   ➢ Includes western Germany only.

| Coefficients used to estimate phosphate from livestock | | |
|---|---|---|
| | kg of dry matter per year | Coefficients for P2O5 content in excrement (% of dry matter) |
| Cattle | 1 500 | 1.8 |
| Horses | 1 200 | 1.4 |
| Sheep and goats | 250 | 0.6 |
| Pigs | 250 | 2.5 |
| Poultry (hens) | 15 | 3.5 |

Source: IEDS-UN/ECE

DNK   ➢ Sales for use in plant production in open agriculture. % change since 1980: base year refer to 1981.
FIN   ➢ Data include forest pesticides and insect repellents.
FRA   ➢ Data refer to quantities sold to agriculture.
DEU   ➢ Data refer to sales.
GRC   ➢ Data refer to sales from wholesale trade to retail trade. % change since 1980: base year refer to 1986.
ITA   ➢ Data refer to formulation weight. % change: base year 1981.
NLD   ➢ Data refer to sales of chemical pesticides. Data include soil disinfectants ,which correspond, for the years presented, to about the half of the total consumption. % change since 1980: base year refer to 1984.
NOR   ➢ Data refer to sales.
PRT   ➢ Data refer to sales.
ESP   ➢ Data refer to sales. % change since 1980: base y. refer to 1986.
SWE   ➢ A special sales tax has been applied to pesticides since 1987. Another tax was applied in 1995. Data refer to sales.
CHE   ➢ Data refer to sales and have been estimated to represent 95 per cent of the total market volume; Liechtenstein included.

TUR ➤ Formulation weight. Powdered sulphur and copper sulphate excluded.

UKD ➤ Great Britain only. % change since 1980: base y. refer to early 1980s. Data include sulphuric acid, which represents approx. 40% (1995) of the total.

## EXPENDITURE

### POLLUTION ABATEMENT AND CONTROL EXPENDITURE

Data source:    OECD

♦ Pollution abatement and control (PAC) expenditure according to the abater principle. PAC activities are defined as purposeful activities aimed directly at the prevention, reduction and elimination of pollution or nuisances arising as a residual of production processes or the consumption of goods and services. Excludes expenditure on natural resource management and activities such as the protection of endangered species, the establishment of natural parks and green belts and activities to exploit natural resources (such as the supply of drinking water).

♦ Total expenditure: the sum of public and business expenditure (excluding households); values in US$ per capita: at current prices and purchasing power parities.

CAN ➤ Estimated 1994 data; public sector: expenditure according to the financing principle.

MEX ➤ Public sector: 1995 partial figure.

USA ➤ 1994 data.

JPN ➤ 1990 data including Secretariat estimate from Environmental Performance Review.

KOR ➤ Trial estimate by the bank of Korea for 1995.

AUS ➤ 1994 data.

AUT ➤ Public sector: 1993 data; business sector and total: 1991 data.

BEL ➤ 1995 data including Brussels; figures refer to regional administrations only; federal and local (municipalities and provinces) administrative levels are excluded.

DNK ➤ 1995 data.

FIN ➤ 1994 data; business sector: ISIC 10 to 40 only (excludes expenditure by private firms specialising in PAC services).

FRA ➤ 1995 data.

DEU ➤ 1994 data for western Germany only.

GRC ➤ 1992 data.

HUN ➤ 1994 data; public and private sectors: investment expenditure only; investments made by organisations with 50 or less employees are included.

ISL ➤ Public sector: 1995 expenditure on waste and waste water only.

ITA ➤ 1989 data.

NLD ➤ 1992 data.

NOR ➤ Secretariat estimate for 1990.

POL ➤ 1995 data; public and private sectors: investment expenditure only.

PRT ➤ 1994 data.

ESP ➤ Public sector: 1993 data; business sector and total: 1991 Secretariat estimate from Environmental Performance Review.

SWE ➤ 1991 data.

CHE ➤ Public sector: 1992 data; business sector and total: 1993 data.

UKD ➤ 1990 data.

### OFFICIAL DEVELOPMENT ASSISTANCE

Data source:    OECD-DAC

♦ Data refer to loans (except military loans), grants and technical co-operation by the public sector to developing countries. Data cover OECD Development Assistance Committee (DAC) Member countries.

## MEMBERS OF THE OECD GROUP ON THE STATE OF THE ENVIRONMENT
### 1997
### CHAIRMAN: Mr. K. TIETMANN

♦ AUSTRALIA — Mr. G. Oakley
Mr. A. Haines (Vice-Chairman)

♦ AUSTRIA — Ms. I. Fiala
Mr. G. Simhandl

♦ BELGIUM — Mr. B. Kestemont
Ms. A. Teller

♦ CANADA — Mr. D. O'Farrell

♦ CZECH Republic — Mr. E. Lippert
Ms. I. Ritschelova

♦ DENMARK — Mr. L. F. Mortensen
Mr. E. Vesselbo

♦ FINLAND — Mr. L. Kolttola
Mr. J. Muurman

♦ FRANCE — Mr. T. Lavoux (Vice-chairman)

♦ GERMANY — Ms. U. Lauber
Mr. K. Tietmann (Chairman)

♦ GREECE — Ms. M. Peppa

♦ HUNGARY — Mr. T. Laszlo
Mr. E. Szabo

♦ ICELAND — Ms. E. Hermannsdottir

♦ IRELAND — Mr. L. Stapleton

♦ ITALY — Mr. C. Constantino
Mr. P. Soprano

♦ JAPAN — Mr. Y. Moriguchi

♦ LUXEMBOURG — Mr. J.P. Feltgen

♦ MEXICO — Mr. G. Gonzales-Davila
Mr. F. Guillen Martin
Mr. Y. Rodriguez Aldabe (Vice-Chairman)

♦ NETHERLANDS — Mr. P. Klein

♦ NORWAY — Mr. O. Nesje
Mr. F. Brunvol

♦ POLAND — Ms. L. Dygas-Ciolkowska
Ms. D. Dziel

♦ PORTUGAL — Mr. P. Nunes Liberato

♦ SPAIN — Mr. N. Olmedo

♦ SWEDEN — Ms. E. Hellsten
Ms. M. Notter

♦ SWITZERLAND — Mr. D. Martin
Mr. P. Grolimund

♦ TURQUIE — Ms. S. Guven

♦ UNITED KINGDOM — Mr. J. Custance

♦ UNITED STATES — Mr. P. Ross (Vice-Chairman)

♦ CEC — Ms. I. Ohman
Mr. T. Van Cruchten
Mr. P. Bosch

## OECD SECRETARIAT

Ms. M. LINSTER
Mr. D. CHOI, Ms. F. ZEGEL

Consultants: Ms. T. COSTA PEREIRA, Mr. A. YAÑEZ

OECD PUBLICATIONS, 2, rue André-Pascal, 75775 PARIS CEDEX 16
PRINTED IN FRANCE
(97 98 03 1 P) ISBN 92-64-16080-9 – No. 50075 1998